Alan **Titchmarsh**
how to garden

Pruning
and Training

Alan Titchmarsh
how to garden

Pruning
and Training

BBC
BOOKS

Published in 2009 by BBC Books, an imprint of
Ebury Publishing, a Random House Group Company

Copyright © Alan Titchmarsh 2009

The right of Alan Titchmarsh to be identified as the
author of this work has been asserted in accordance
with Sections 77 and 78 of the Copyright, Designs and
Patents Act 1988.

The Random House Group Limited Reg. No. 954009

Addresses for companies within the Random House
Group can be found at:
www.randomhouse.co.uk

The Random House Group Limited supports The Forest
Stewardship Council (FSC), the leading international
forest certification organisation. All our titles that are
printed on Greenpeace approved FSC certified paper
carry the FSC logo. Our paper procurement policy can
be found at www.rbooks.co.uk/environment

A CIP catalogue record for this book is available from
the British Library.

ISBN 978-1-84-6074004

Produced by Outhouse!
Shalbourne, Marlborough, Wiltshire SN8 3QJ

BBC BOOKS
COMMISSIONING EDITORS: Lorna Russell, Stuart Cooper
PROJECT EDITOR: Caroline McArthur
PRODUCTION CONTROLLER: Bridget Fish, Antony Heller

OUTHOUSE!
CONCEPT DEVELOPMENT & PROJECT MANAGEMENT:
   Elizabeth Mallard-Shaw
CONTRIBUTING EDITOR: Steve Bradley
EDITOR: Alison Copland
ART DIRECTION: Heather McCarry
SERIES DESIGN: Sharon Cluett
DESIGNER: Heather McCarry

ILLUSTRATIONS by Lizzie Harper

PHOTOGRAPHS by Jonathan Buckley, except where
credited otherwise on page 144

Colour origination, printed and bound by
Firmengruppe APPL, Wemding, Germany

**Essex County
Council Libraries**

Contents

Introduction

Gardening is one of the best and most fulfilling activities on earth, but it can sometimes seem complicated and confusing. The answers to problems can usually be found in books, but big fat gardening books can be rather daunting. Where do you start? How can you find just the information you want without wading through lots of stuff that is not appropriate to your particular problem? Well, a good index is helpful, but sometimes a smaller book devoted to one particular subject fits the bill better – especially if it is reasonably priced and if you have a small garden where you might not be able to fit in everything suggested in a larger volume.

The *How to Garden* books aim to fill that gap – even if sometimes it may be only a small one. They are clearly set out and written, I hope, in a straightforward, easy-to-understand style. I don't see any point in making gardening complicated, when much of it is based on common sense and observation. (All the key techniques are explained and illustrated, and I've included plenty of tips and tricks of the trade.)

There are suggestions on the best plants and the best varieties to grow in particular situations and for a particular effect. I've tried to keep the information crisp and to the point so that you can find what you need quickly and easily and then put your new-found knowledge into practice. Don't worry if you're not familiar with the Latin names of plants. They are there to make sure you can find the plant as it will be labelled in the nursery or garden centre, but where appropriate I have included common names, too. Forgetting a plant's name need not stand in your way when it comes to being able to grow it.

Above all, the *How to Garden* books are designed to fill you with passion and enthusiasm for your garden and all that its creation and care entails, from designing and planting it to maintaining it and enjoying it. For more than fifty years gardening has been my passion, and that initial enthusiasm for watching plants grow, for trying something new and for just being outside pottering has never faded. If anything I am keener on gardening now than I ever was and get more satisfaction from my plants every day. It's not that I am simply a romantic, but rather that I have learned to look for the good in gardens and in plants, and there is lots to be found. Oh, there are times when I fail – when my plants don't grow as well as they should and I need to try harder. But where would I rather be on a sunny day? Nowhere!

The *How to Garden* handbooks will, I hope, allow some of that enthusiasm – childish though it may be – to rub off on you, and the information they contain will, I hope, make you a better gardener, as well as opening your eyes to the magic of plants and flowers.

Principles and purpose

Successful pruning is not the mystical art that it might sometimes appear to be. It does, however, require an understanding of why pruning is necessary. Most mistakes and failures happen when someone decides to 'do a bit of pruning' because a couple of shrubs need a haircut, and before you know it everything in the garden has been given a short back and sides. Pruning without purpose does more harm than good, so careful preparation and knowing what you want to achieve are both vitally important.

What is pruning?

Pruning has been described as the removal of parts of a plant for a particular purpose, but it's not usually that simple. Often there will be several objectives rather than just one. Before you prune anything, you must have an idea of what you hope to achieve and how the plant should respond. Knowing how it will look once the pruning is complete (and through the coming seasons) should influence what you do.

Some plants can be left largely to their own devices and will still grow reasonably well. After all, many trees and shrubs grow happily in the wild and are never pruned, although you might want to cut them back a little to suit the size and shape of your garden. At the other end of the spectrum, some plants are constantly clipped – often two or three times each season, in the case of topiary – resulting in amazing garden 'sculptures'. Generally, though, a bit of routine pruning is beneficial for plants; to improve their health, vigour, performance and shape or to restrict its size (*see* pages 10–12).

Remember that pruning will not solve all of the growth, performance and habit problems a plant may experience, and no amount of pruning will ever correct or control a plant when it's growing in the wrong place. For instance, a large tree may have to be cut back severely on an annual basis, to the

point where it bears no resemblance to its true natural form and habit, simply because it has been planted too close to a house or building. Similarly, a hedge of the highly vigorous × *Cupressocyparis leylandii* (Leyland cypress) will never look right in a small suburban garden, no matter how often it's cut back, and it will dwarf and shade neighbouring plants in no time.

Always use the right tools. Secateurs are fine for smaller stems, but never strain them. Use loppers and pruning saws for larger stems or branches.

These are both examples of the wrong plant in the wrong place and, sadly, the only realistic solution is to remove them and replace them with other plants that are more suited to the surroundings.

Why prune?

There are a number of reasons for pruning: to encourage strong, healthy growth, to increase flower or fruit production, and to create a more pleasing, balanced shape and restrict growth. Pruning can also perform a more specialized function – you can use pruning techniques to train young trees and shrubs, or to create special effects such as coloured stems or large leaves in certain species. Some plants need regular attention to give of their best, while others may require only an annual trim or some formative pruning in their early years.

Even established trees benefit from pruning; removing weak, spindly or crossing branches will improve health and appearance. Raising or thinning crowns also increases the light level for plants growing below.

Health and vigour

Pruning trees and shrubs for health and vigour involves removing shoots, branches, stems or leaves that will have a detrimental effect on the plant if they are left alone. Parts of a plant that are infected with fungal disease or that have died back should be taken out as soon as possible in order to prevent problems increasing and affecting healthy tissue.

Overcrowded plants are prone to attack by fungal diseases because the air flow through the branches is reduced, and where shoots rub together in the wind it creates an open wound through which spores can enter and attack. Pruning trees and shrubs to remove any stems or branches whose woody tissue has been invaded by fungal or bacterial diseases can (if done in time) prevent the spread of many diseases and often prolong the life of the plant. Removing thin, weak, spindly shoots, which are most vulnerable to attack, and thinning out the growth in the centre of a plant to allow a good flow of air around the branches, both help to make life more difficult for diseases such as mildews and pests such as aphids, thus reducing the need for spraying.

With some plants, if a branch or stem has been twisted, broken or split as a result of wind or other damage (for instance, soft shoots being killed by frost or wind chill), the wound almost always gets infected or becomes a sheltering site for pests that may attack other parts of the plant. Here, pruning is used to remove the damaged growth before the attack can progress. The plant may take several years to recover and regain its natural shape afterwards, but a sacrifice made in the short term can extend the life span of the remaining parts of the plant.

Shaping

It is necessary to prune some woody plants constantly throughout their lives to maintain their habit. This can range from the occasional cutting back of a few stems to retain an attractive form, to regular and essential trimming of more complex shapes. The most obvious example of the latter is in topiary, when clipping

What happens if you don't prune?

Some trees and shrubs will grow quite happily without regular pruning, although in the average garden some pruning will probably be necessary to keep the plant under control. Few gardens have sufficient space for a tree to be allowed to grow entirely unchecked.

However, often when plants are left to grow naturally without any pruning, they develop faults that can lead to the production of misshapen shoots and stems. These may result in further damage later in the plant's life. This problem is quite common with trees and shrubs where branches develop too closely together – branches rub together, causing injury, or narrow forks form, which are prone to splits and breaks when the stems become larger. Even a plant such as magnolia, which often needs very little pruning once established, will benefit from pruning and training as a young plant to prevent any of these common faults developing.

Maintenance pruning can also reduce the risk of damage to a plant from pests and diseases, by creating the type of conditions that make the plant less prone to attack.

plants into a particular shape. For instance: a cone, a sphere or a spiral, or more elaborate creations such as bird or animal forms – such plants become living statues (*see* below and pages 68–71). Hedges may also need to be clipped or trimmed regularly (up to three times a year) to maintain their shape (*see* pages 64–5).

Balance

Young plants, especially woody ones, tend to produce lots of strong vigorous growth. This is followed by a period of fairly balanced growth, with equal energy going into both flower and fruit production and leaf and shoot development. Later, as the plant ages, there is a greater emphasis on flowers and fruit, with much less new leaf and shoot growth.

One of the main purposes of pruning is to keep a balance between the two types of growth. Some pruning each year may be necessary

Some plants, such as shrubby willows (*Salix*) or dogwoods (here, *Cornus alba* 'Sibirica') are best pruned hard every year in early spring. They respond by producing a crop of bright young stems that make a vivid display in winter.

to encourage more flowers and fruit in the early stages of the plant's life. As the plant matures, the emphasis will shift towards encouraging new shoots to form to replace older ones, to sustain the plant. It is easy to forget that flowering and fruiting can often put a huge strain on a plant, and so it needs sufficient green leaves to manufacture food to support it during this period.

Special effects

You can use pruning techniques to create a variety of special ornamental effects. For instance, some plants respond to annual hard pruning by producing stunning new shoots

or leaves. If hard pruned, *Cotinus coggygria* 'Royal Purple' (purple-leaved smoke bush) and *Sambucus nigra* f. *laciniata* (cut-leaved elderberry) will produce a few stems with very large, brightly coloured leaves – these are popular with flower arrangers, who use their impressive foliage as background 'greenery' in their displays. *Corylus avellana* 'Contorta' (contorted or corkscrew hazel) and some dogwoods (*Salix* or *Cornus* species) respond to hard pruning by producing striking twisted stems or brightly coloured young shoots respectively (*see* above and pages 54).

Pruning for effect can also involve

Topiary is the triumph of the gardener (armed with pruning shears) over nature. These gigantic and fantastical coffee pots are the result of decades of regular trimming.

altering the growth habit of a plant to suit a particular situation. For instance, a flowering quince (*Chaenomeles*) or a pyracantha can be grown as a freestanding shrub in a border, or – if pruned differently – the same plant may be grown successfully as a wall shrub (*see* page 48) or a hedge (*see* page 64).

Fruit and flower production

With many wall shrubs, climbing plants and fruit trees, pruning and tying growths into set positions will maximize the quantity of flowers or healthy, undamaged fruit, as well as limit the amount of growth a plant produces each year.

A fruiting plant left to its own devices will usually produce large amounts of small fruits. By pruning to reduce the number of stems, you can direct the plant's energy into making fewer, larger fruits. This,

Many wall shrubs (*see* pages 48–9) need pruning to encourage the stems to grow up and along the wall, rather than outwards. This peach (*Prunus persica* 'Peregrine') has been trained into a fan shape.

coupled with the practice of 'fruit thinning', to remove a proportion of the fruits where overcrowding has occurred, can be used to improve fruit size and quality.

To produce a good crop of fruit from trees growing in a confined space, fruit growers prune and train the trees into specific shapes, such as cordons, espaliers and fans (*see* pages 42–3 and above).

Size restriction

The size of a plant can be controlled by regularly pruning out shoots. However, this is an ongoing process that must be repeated frequently,

Many plants, including wisteria (here, *W. floribunda* 'Alba') flower better when they are trained horizontally. Make sure the wall can take the weight – the flowering branches can be very heavy.

and one that does not in itself slow or restrict the plant's growth. For this, you need to root-prune (*see* page 116). Cutting through the roots of a plant checks the flow of water and nutrients to the stems, thereby limiting the growth potential of the plant and consequently its height and spread. (Bonsai could be considered the ultimate example of effective root pruning combined with regular trimming.)

To produce the desired effect, root pruning can be carried out in one operation or in stages. Either way, it will slow the plant's growth for several years, after which it may need to be repeated.

Vertical and horizontal growth

Many plants display a characteristic known as apical dominance, where the growing tip (apex) of a shoot dominates the growth of that stem. No side (or 'lateral') shoots develop in the area immediately below the growing point and the result is a very slender, vertical plant. This isn't always desirable, for several reasons: bushier, fuller growth may be required, and in some cases horizontal branches produce better flowers or fruit. The problem of apical dominance can be overcome by pruning.

To create bushy, multi-branched plants you need to break apical dominance, either by bending a stem into a horizontal position (*see* below) or by removing the shoot tip (*see* right). The former reduces the flow of sap to the terminal bud and the latter stops sap flow completely. Both methods will lead to the growth of sideshoots, along with a new growing point (usually from the highest bud). With young plants, removing the tip is often referred to as 'pinching' or 'pinching out' – you can either snap off the tender shoot tip between your finger and thumb, or cut it off with a sharp knife. With woody plants, you should cut off the growing point (and often part of the stem, too) using a pair of sharp secateurs.

Horizontal shoots

Many climbing plants can be coaxed into better flower development and producing more shoots by bending the long, trailing growths down into a horizontal position and tying them in place. This will have the effect of encouraging flower buds to form along the entire length of the shoot, rather than just on the growing point. It is no coincidence that when you see wisteria growing on house walls it is invariably the horizontal branches that are covered in flowers (*see* opposite).

Fruit growers increase the yield of their apple trees using this technique; tying new young shoots into a horizontal position encourages fruit buds to form along the entire length of the shoots, while also allowing more sunlight to reach the fruit, since the branches are evenly spaced. The end product is fruit that is better coloured and easier to see and pick. These horizontal shoots need to be tied into this position for only one or two years until they become woody and fixed in position. They then remain horizontal, but any new shoots that form as extensions of these will try to grow vertically again, so you will need to train these horizontally or prune them out.

Apical dominance can be broken in two ways, with slightly different effects:
① Removing the tender growing tip from young plants or shoots to encourage the plant to branch outwards.
② Bending a stem until it is horizontal to encourage the growth of more sideshoots.

Types of pruning

There are four main types of pruning: formative, maintenance (or routine), renewal, and renovation (or rejuvenation). The type of pruning you decide to do will depend on what you want to achieve, the type of plant you are pruning, and the plant's stage of development. As a general rule, younger plants need more pruning in order to create a good framework of branches and stems.

Formative pruning

This is used mainly for young or developing plants. The aim is to create even growth and overall development, but it can also be used to shape plants into a particular structural framework. Even plants that you intend to grow 'naturally' (so that they follow their normal growth habit) need some pruning in the early stages to prevent problems later on. For instance, if you don't prune a tree when it is young, it may form narrow-angled branches, which are very vulnerable to splitting as the plant gets older. Also, some trees and shrubs that have their buds in opposite pairs have a strong tendency to develop into 'forked' stems – where two buds at the top of a shoot grow at an equal rate. They eventually create a narrow fork that can easily split, and this can lead to half of the crown or top of the plant being lost if one shoot breaks. Again, formative pruning will reduce the chances of forked stems occurring.

The amount of formative pruning you undertake depends to a large extent on the type of plant and the way in which it has been grown in its early years. For example, if

Work put in when a plant is young yields long-lasting results. A standard bay (*Laurus nobilis*) is not difficult to produce, but it does take patience.

you've propagated a plant yourself you'll need to train it from scratch. However, if you buy a container-grown fruit tree or shrub that has been partially trained from a garden centre or nursery, there will be very little formative pruning to do because the work has been started for you.

Standard plants

Possibly the most common form of formative pruning is the creation of 'standards', where a plant (usually

Many trees, including this crab apple (*Malus*), will have a more attractive shape if they are pruned when young. Remove the lowest branches to give a clear trunk, cut out any badly placed shoots, and shorten leggy growth.

a tree) is trained on a single stem (or 'leg') with a cluster of branches (or 'head') at the top (*see* page 60). Sometimes the stem and head are of the same plant, or they may be different varieties. In the case of a 'weeping' standard, the top is often a trailing ground-cover plant that has been grafted onto a straight stem to create the effect. With these types of plant a separate pruning regime is required for each stage of the plant's development; one type of formative pruning is used to create the stem and another to form the head.

Maintenance pruning

As the name suggests, this is the type of pruning carried out to keep plants healthy and growing and performing in the way you want them to. This type of pruning (also known as routine pruning) is aimed at retaining a balance between growth and flowering or fruiting.

Some plants, such as *Brachyglottis* (syn. *Senecio*), *Callistemon* (bottle brush), *Hebe* and lavender (*see* below), have a natural tendency to become bare and 'leggy' at the base so they are routinely pruned after flowering to shorten the top growth. This allows plenty of light into the base of the plant and encourages shoots to form lower down the stems. Many of these shrubs thrive in plenty of light, and one of the main reasons for them developing a sparse growth habit with bare wood at the base is because of top growth shading the lower levels of the plant and causing the foliage to die.

Other forms of maintenance pruning include dead-heading (removing old flowers, *see* page 30) and removing unwanted suckers (*see* page 33).

Renewal pruning

This technique is often used for pruning established fruit trees, but it can also be used on established shrubs where minimal pruning is required. It involves very little cutting but it will help keep established plants growing well. Renewal pruning involves the removal of older growth to make room for new shoots to grow as replacements; fruit growers often refer to it as 'replacement' pruning.

Ornamental cherries and apples

Many ornamental cherries can also be pruned in this way, particularly those that produce flowers only on the shoot tips. If you prune these plants overall to stop them spreading too far, you will be removing flower-bearing wood each time. By removing complete branches and making way for other branches to grow naturally, and creating room for replacement shoots, only a small amount of flower is lost. This strikes a balance between losing some flowering wood and allowing other shoots to form that will bear future generations of flowers.

Apple trees with a tip-bearing (or partially tip-bearing) habit, such as the cooking apple *Malus domestica* 'Bramley's Seedling' (*see* page 16), often crop better when pruned by this method.

Some plants become scruffy and short-lived when left to grow naturally. Lavender should be shorn back to low buds in spring to keep it compact and looking neat.

Unlike most apples, which flower and fruit on spurs along the branch, the classic 'Bramley's Seedling' produces its fruit towards the tips of the branches.

shoots of similar size and thickness. In this case, renewal pruning consists of cutting out a number of shoots each year (usually the oldest and most unproductive) with a saw or loppers, as close to ground level as possible, to create space for new, vigorous replacement shoots. No other pruning is normally required, other than trimming any shoots that are damaged when the large stems are removed. If this regime is followed regularly, after four to five years all the older shoots will have been replaced by new ones.

Renovation (rejuvenation)

Whichever word you use, this type of pruning amounts to the same thing: implementing a severe pruning regime to give a misshapen, overgrown, tired and neglected plant a new lease of life. In short, it is the rescue operation that you attempt when the only other option is to remove the plant and start again. However, as with most things in the life of a gardener, success is not guaranteed and, with some plants, failure is inevitable. Conifers seldom regrow if you prune into old, brown growth; the exceptions are *Taxus baccata* (English yew) and *Thuja plicata* (western red cedar), which will both recover. As a general rule, conifers are usually replaced rather than hard pruned. Several other plants are also unable to come back from this type of pruning –

Weeping trees

Renewal pruning is very useful as a method for pruning plants with a weeping habit, where the newer shoots tend to emerge and arch over previous generations of branches. The problem with this type of growth habit is that the older branches become shaded by the newer, stronger shoots and suffer from a lack of light. The growth becomes weak or dies off and large quantities of dead or dying wood

can accumulate, which may harbour pests and diseases. Where this is the case, simply remove the lower, older shoots and branches; this will either allow in sufficient sunlight to encourage new shoots to emerge, or create enough room for the younger shoots to spread and grow naturally.

Ornamental shrubs

A number of ornamental shrubs can be renewal pruned, because these tend to form a dense clump of mainly broad-leaved evergreens such as *Ceanothus, Coronilla, Cytisus, Genista, Lavandula* and *Santolina*.

If a plant is a suitable candidate for renovation (*see* below), it is worth having a go, especially if the plant is valuable or otherwise difficult to replace. If it is healthy and vigorous, albeit neglected, it should respond. If it does not, dig it out and replace it.

Renovating gradually

Renovation must be carried out in stages: it is not an overnight mission, so it does require patience. It will usually involve cutting back (hard) half of the plant one year and the other half the following year, so it may be two or three years before you see the plant really start to look happy again. Flowering may take a year longer. With a hedge, the need to renovate in stages is a great advantage because it means you can keep a certain amount of privacy and shelter while the plants recover.

If the plant responds well to the first year's pruning it will produce a quantity of strong, vigorous shoots. In some cases there may be far too many new shoots for your intended purpose. They may also (inevitably!) grow in completely the wrong place, and usually all together. So part of the second stage of renovation is to select for retention those new shoots that will produce a strong, well-balanced plant and to 'thin out' or remove the others (always remove the spindliest, weakest shoots first).

If at the end of it all you find that your rescue mission has been a success, the effort will have been worthwhile. For a gardener, it is enormously satisfying to see a much-loved but neglected plant restored to its former glory.

Rejuvenate large plants like this *Magnolia × loebneri* 'Leonard Messel' and *Camellia japonica* 'Mercury' by cutting back over two or three years.

Plants suitable for renovation pruning

Abeliophyllum

Aucuba

Callistemon

Calycanthus

Camellia

Carpenteria

Chaenomeles

Chimonanthus

Cornus

Cotoneaster

Daphne

Eucryphia

Garrya

Hydrangea anomala subsp. petiolaris

Ilex

Kalmia

Magnolia × soulangeana

Mahonia × media

Malus

Osmanthus

Pyrus

Rhododendron

Schizophragma

Wisteria

Getting started

Before you whip out your pruning loppers, decide what it is you're trying to achieve. Ask yourself why you are pruning the plant and what you expect from it after it has been pruned. Next, you need to make sure that you have the equipment to do the job and that it is in excellent condition. Hacking away at stems with rusty or blunt tools will cause more damage than just about anything else.

Planning your pruning

It is easy to forget that pruning provokes growth, and the way you prune will determine how the plant responds. With any type of pruning, you can divide it up into the cuts you *need* to make (necessary cuts, or the 'four Ds') and the cuts you *would like* to make (desirable cuts).

The cuts you *need* to make are those that protect the health and well-being of the plant you're pruning. The cuts you *would like* to make are those that will shape or form the plant – these are the cuts that will influence the growth and general performance of the plant.

Choosing the right tool

First, decide which tool is most appropriate for the task. The tool you use will depend on the thickness of the stem or branch that you're intending to cut, and it's quite possible you'll need at least two cutting implements to cope with the difference in stem size and thickness. For woody shoots up to 1cm (½in) thick, use secateurs. For thick, woody shoots 1–2.5cm (½–1in) thick, and for inaccessible stems, long-handled pruners, or loppers, are ideal. For very thick branches you'll need to use a pruning saw. A garden knife is also useful for light pruning tasks. (For information on tools, *see* pages 22–5.)

Necessary cuts

There are some basic rules to follow when you start pruning any plant, and these should make the task of pruning easier. First, inspect your plant and make decisions about what to remove and what to leave. The essential parts to cut out are known as the 'four Ds', which makes them easier to remember:

- Dead
- Damaged
- Diseased
- Dying

The four Ds are all necessary cuts and should always be carried out before any other pruning. There is nothing more annoying than doing quite a bit of work on a stem or branch only to find that it is diseased at the base and should have been cut out at ground level or where it meets the main trunk.

Dead wood

First, remove any dead branches from the plant you're pruning. Dead wood makes no contribution at all to the plant and will form a perfect site for the eggs of insect pests and spores of fungal diseases to survive the winter successfully and emerge to attack the plant in the following spring.

The dead wood may be hard and dry so, wherever possible, remove it with a saw – cutting through it with secateurs or loppers can be very hard work and will quickly blunt your tools (this is because they are designed to cut through live, green, sappy wood). With some plants it's very difficult to tell which stems are dead and which are alive, especially if you are pruning in the winter when the plants are dormant. If in doubt, do the scrape test (*see* Don't forget, below).

Using the right tool for the job is vital. If you tackle thick stems like the ones of this dogwood (*Cornus*) with secateurs, you'll mash up the stems (and probably damage the blades into the bargain).

Don't forget

Whenever you are not sure if a shoot is alive, there is a simple but effective test you can do. Scrape away a small amount of bark with your fingernail or a clean knife. If the wood below the bark is a greenish white, there is a very good chance that the growth in this area is still alive. If you find dry, brown or grey wood under the bark, the area you have exposed is almost certainly dead. You can repeat this process along a stem or branch to find out the extent of the dead areas. (Not all plants have greenish-white live tissue under the bark: berberis, magnolias and mahonias all have live tissue that is orange or yellow.)

Alternatively, you could wait until growth starts, when it will be much easier to distinguish between live shoots and dead ones.

Damaged branches and stems

Plants with damaged branches and stems are difficult to make a decision about, mainly because you need to determine what degree of damage you are prepared to accept and what is severe enough to need to be removed for the health of the plant.

Where branches and stems are broken, make a pruning cut into healthy wood below the damaged area. A split stem exposes the inner tissue, and this type of wound very rarely heals because it is continually opening and closing every time the branch or stem moves. It is vulnerable to the entry of fungal spores, which can eventually cause the entire plant to die.

The difficulty comes where the damage has been caused to stems and branches by rubbing or scraping – either two branches rubbing together, or where stems and branches are rubbing against some type of foreign body, such as a tree touching its supporting stake and ties or, most often, climbers and wall shrubs chafing against a wall, fence, or other support structure when the wind is blowing. Any form of damage will tend to create an open wound that, particularly with rubbing, never gets the chance to heal because it is constantly being reopened. A large amount of the plant's energy will be diverted into producing callus (healing tissue) in an attempt to close the wound.

With wounds on climbing plants and trees where the injury is caused by contact with the supports or ties, the very least you need to do is re-tie stems and branches so that they are no longer loose. If the damage is severe, some pruning will be needed to remove the damaged parts.

Diseased growth

You will need to remove any branch, shoot or root that shows signs of disease (or severe pest infestation) in an attempt to safeguard the remaining parts of the plant. This may involve paring away some bark with a sharp knife to remove the early signs of a disease attack or, in a lot of cases, taking away complete branches to halt the progressive spread of a fungus or bacterium. The main problem is knowing how much to remove. It is best to remove as little growth as possible, but it is also important to be sure you have eradicated the problem completely.

In many cases, branches and stems that are being attacked by fungal or bacterial diseases will give clues to their rate of progress if you know

Leaves and stems that are affected by diseases should be removed as soon as they are spotted.

where to look. For instance, you may see a coloured staining in the wood, which may be present just under the bark or running through the centre of the stem. The best way to be sure you have removed all traces of infection is to cut back beyond these areas of staining in the hope that you have removed all the diseased parts.

Dying parts

Wilting shoots and leaves or peeling bark are often signs that a plant, or a section of a plant, is dying. It is well worth pruning these sections out as a precaution, but don't just leave it there – always investigate further to see if you can identify the cause. The main justification for removing any shoots you think are dying is to try to prevent any infection spreading through the plant. Diseases such as coral spot fungus will establish on dead shoots and twigs and then start to invade the living parts of a plant.

To encourage the annual production of colourful stems in shrubs such as this *Cornus alba* (dogwood), you need to hard prune in spring (*see* page 54).

Desirable cuts

When all the necessary cuts have been made, you can begin to prune your plants for appearance. Always start with a plan and have some idea of what the plant should look like

This single-tier espalier apple on a dwarfing rootstock creates a low step-over hedge. Having apples growing close to the ground can be convenient, but can also attract ground-living pests.

when you have finished. You should also know what you want the plant to do – for instance, if you want more flowers, prune accordingly.

Where the plants' overall appearance is more important than flowering, particularly where they are being grown as hedges or for topiary, try to imagine each plant after it has responded to being pruned. Hard pruning encourages strong, vigorous growth, but this is frequently at the expense of flowers – at least during the first season after pruning, and sometimes even longer.

When you prune or train a plant, the main objective is to improve the performance of that plant. This can be for better foliage colour, brightly coloured stems, more or larger flowers, or more or better fruit. When you do this, though, you always need to consider the plant as a whole, rather than focus solely on one aspect. A plant cannot thrive and give you large, delicious fruits every year if you keep cutting the leaves off, or if you prune off all of the shoots that are producing flower-bearing growths for the following year.

Don't forget

Pruning often has to strike a balance between how you would like your plant to grow now and its appearance in future seasons. It is much easier to work with a plant's natural growth habit rather than trying to force it to develop in a totally unnatural way.

Tools for the job

Knives, secateurs, loppers, saws and extending-reach pruners all have their uses when pruning, with shears and clippers being used for trimming hedges and topiary. Having the correct tool for the task makes working much easier and produces considerably better results.

Hand tools

You will need a decent set of hand tools for carrying out the wide range of pruning tasks in the garden. It is well worth investing in good-quality equipment at the outset.

Pruning knife

A pruning knife is a heavy knife with a curved blade that enables you to get a 'slicing' action when cutting. The handle is also curved, or has a bulbous base, to give a better grip. It is used mainly for light trimming or finishing off cuts made with a saw, such as trimming ragged bark.

Secateurs

For most types of lighter pruning, including cutting woody shoots up to approximately 1cm (½in) thick,

the best tool is a pair of sharp, well-maintained secateurs. There are two basic types, which vary in their cutting action. 'Bypass' secateurs have two curved metal blades that pass one another very closely and cut rather like a pair of scissors. 'Anvil' types have a single, straight-edged cutting blade that closes down onto an anvil (a bar of softer metal or plastic), giving a guillotine-like cutting action.

Some anvil-type secateurs have been designed to incorporate a ratchet. The blades can be locked into position around the branch, and then the ratchet is released to cut through the branch in stages. These are good for gardeners with a small hand span, but they have a relatively slow cutting action.

A pruning knife is perfect for cutting soft stems or for tidying up saw cuts.

Shears

These are long-bladed pruners, also known as 'clippers'. All have a bypass cutting action and are intended mainly for cutting hedges or lawns, with the longer cutting blades covering an larger area quickly. Often the handles are of similar length to the blades and they are joined together at a central pivotal point. They should be well balanced, strong,

Anvil and bypass secateurs

All secateur types can produce good, healthy cuts if they are used correctly. However, anvil-type secateurs (see below left) are not suitable for plants with hollow or brittle stems because their guillotine-like cutting action can crush the stems and cause damage.

In the case of hollow- or brittle-stemmed plants, use bypass secateurs (see below right), which cause less crushing and bruising. This will also reduce the risk of shoots dying back. Don't stint when buying secateurs; a sturdy pair, well maintained, can last a lifetime.

Anvil secateurs

Bypass secateurs

Loppers make the best job of thick, woody stems. The blades are larger than those of secateurs and the long handles make the job less strenuous.

Long-handled pruners (loppers)

These are basically strong secateurs with long handles that give extra leverage when cutting stems or branches that are too thick to be tackled with secateurs – for branches about 1–2.5cm (½–1in) thick. The cutting mechanism can be either bypass or anvil type, and there are a few variations on the basic design: some have a ratchet, to make it possible to cut in stages, and others have a gear mechanism on the blade and handle to provide extra leverage and make cutting easier. Versions with extending handles, to increase leverage, are also available (see page 24).

Pruning saw

These saws are intended for use on stems and branches that are too large for loppers to cut through – that is, branches that are more than about 2.5cm (1in) thick. There are three main types: single-edged, double-edged and bow saws.

Some single-edged saws have a fixed, straight blade. Many of these are designed to fold, or retract, so that the blade closes back into the handle (like a penknife), and the saw fits neatly into a pocket when not in use. Others have a slightly curved blade – these are based on the 'Grecian saw', which has a curved blade and sloping teeth. Both are designed to cut on the pull stroke. Most taper to a sharp point,

which makes them very useful for getting access to small spaces in the narrow angles between branches.

The traditional double-edged pruning saw has a tapering blade with a broad, blunt end and teeth on both sides. One side has small teeth for cutting through dry, dead wood, while the other has much coarser teeth designed to cut cleanly through living, wet, sappy wood.

Bow saws have a sprung metal frame, curved in the shape of a bow, holding a wide blade with coarse teeth. The blade is held under tension by the frame to make cutting easier. This type of saw gives a rough cut and is intended for cutting through larger branches and trunks (it was originally designed for sawing logs). There is also a smaller version called a half-bow saw, with the metal frame tapering to a sharp point at one end; this is used for cutting through smaller branches and working in situations where space is restricted. Bow saws cut on the push stroke.

light and comfortable to use. Most have straight blades with a deep notch at the base of the blade for cutting thicker stems.

Some shears have a blade with a wavy edge, which acts to trap the shoots being cut through and thereby give a cleaner cut. It is also possible to get 'one-handed' or 'single-handed' models, in which the blades are operated by squeezing a lever against the handle to open and close the blades, but these tend to have small blades and are suitable only for light trimming.

Tool maintenance

All tools need to be frequently maintained to keep them operating efficiently and comfortably. Oil all moving parts regularly and when blades become clogged with dry sap, rub them clean with emery paper. When the blades become blunt they may be sharpened, either on an oilstone or, in the case of powered tools, sent in for servicing.

The pruning saw – essential for making clean cuts in stems that are too thick for loppers to cope with.

Long-arm pruners

These are 'loppers on a pole' and consist of a pole 2–3m (6–10ft) in length, with a hooked end and curved blade at the tip; the blade is operated by a lever or pull toggle at the opposite end. These tools are more specialized and are used for pruning tree branches that would normally be out of reach (unless a ladder or stepladder is used), and some are capable of cutting through branches up to 4cm (1½in) thick. Some models have extending poles, and there is at least one version with a set of shear blades attached – these are designed for clipping tall hedges from a ground-level position.

Pole saw

A pole saw consists of a fixed or extending pole 2–3m (6–10ft) in length, with a saw attachment fitted to the tip. The saw is usually a curved Grecian type that cuts on the 'pull' stroke, which is much easier for pruning over head height. These are used for pruning tree branches that would normally be too high to reach without a ladder or stepladder.

Powered tools

Where you plan to undertake large amounts of very similar types of pruning – perhaps clipping a large hedge – powered tools can save a lot of work (see also pages 26–7).

Cutter-bar hedge trimmer

This involves a scissor-like action of either one moving (reciprocating) blade and one fixed blade trapping and severing the stems, or two moving blades cutting through the shoots. These trimmers have a cutter bar onto which the moving blades are fixed, and usually cut on both sides of the cutter bar; there are models that will cut on only one side, and these are usually the ones that are capable of cutting through thicker material.

These trimmers can be powered by various means. Petrol is used in heavier machines, which are ideal for cutting through thicker shoots. These are often favoured by professional gardeners. Mains electricity is at present the most

Battery-operated hedge trimmers are useful for topiary. They are cordless, light, and easy to manoeuvre.

common power source. Most machines are lightweight and give a good-quality finish, but the cable can be a restriction in terms of both mobility and safety (see page 27).

Rechargeable batteries are increasing in popularity – this is mainly because of advances in battery technology, lighter batteries with a longer working life and rapid recharging, and freedom of movement. There is also an increasing range of lightweight trimmers that can be safely held and operated in one hand. These are designed for light work, such as trimming the soft new growths on plants trained as topiary.

Rotary hedge trimmer

This tool is relatively new and quite different from the traditional mechanical hedge trimmers used by home gardeners. Rotating blades are enclosed within a mesh grid that allows the plant stems to protrude through; they are then severed and shredded by the blades rotating at high speed. Rotary trimmers also

Long-arm pruners are a simple but effective way of reaching high branches.

have a 'cassette' fitted behind the blades to collect the prunings, which are chopped down to a tenth of their original volume. At present, all available models are powered by mains electricity.

Telescopic hedge trimmer

These trimmers (*see* below) usually consist of cutter-bar trimmers on the end of an extendable (occasionally fixed) pole, often providing an extra reach of up to 3m (10ft). The cutting head or bar can be adjusted through a range of angles. This variety of movement enables the user to cut both the sides and top of the hedge from a standing position. These machines usually have their power source on the opposite end of the pole from the handle, to balance the overall weight of the engine and cutter.

Again, these can be powered by various means. Petrol-powered trimmers are ideal for really heavy-duty work and where large areas of hedge may need trimming, or where electricity supply may be a problem. These tend to be much heavier machines and are often very noisy. Mains electricity is the most popular power source, with cables plugging into the base of the telescopic arm. Most are lightweight, but the trailing cable can be a hazard.

With rechargeable batteries, the cutting unit and extending pole are quite light. However, the battery unit can be heavy, so with many of these trimmers the battery is fixed to a belt and fitted around the user's waist to distribute the weight more evenly and reduce fatigue.

Pole pruner

The cutting action of a pole pruner is usually chainsaw-like, with linked, sharpened saw teeth driven around a fixed guide bar; some types of pole pruner have a circular cutting blade with a high-speed toothed disc. These can be used for trimming branches on trees or thicker stems on neglected hedges or tall shrubs. These devices can have fixed or telescopic poles, usually with a drive unit at the base to counterbalance the guide bar and a chain or disc on the other end.

Some of the chainsaw types can be detached from the pole and used as small chainsaws for work at ground level.

For heavy work, petrol-driven engines provide the power; both mains electric and rechargeable batteries can also be used, although the battery-powered units tend to be smaller and have a limited work time from each charge. Some of the petrol-powered units can be used to prune plants at ground level, particularly where shrubs and dense thickets of woody growth need cutting down.

Nylon-line trimmer (strimmer)

This machine can be used to prune ground-cover plants that are cut down to soil level on a regular basis. A central spool or 'head' rotates at high speed, and the cutting is done either by a spinning disc with 'teeth' around the edge, or by a length of nylon cord.

Chainsaw

A chainsaw is useful for sawing large branches and for major felling jobs. There are electric and petrol-driven models. They can be dangerous, so they should always be operated by someone who has been trained to use them (*see* page 27).

For large areas of hedge, particularly high hedges, an extendable, telescopic hedge trimmer is ideal.

Protective clothing and safety

Pruning can be a dangerous undertaking: it involves using sharp tools – often powered – and if you're not careful you may find yourself balancing on a wobbly stepladder placed on uneven ground. If you plan to use a stepladder, make sure there is someone with you to hold it stable. Take good care when bending and stretching, and wear protective clothing to prevent injuries from prickly plants and sharp branches.

Sap from *Euphorbia* plants is an irritant. Protect hands with gloves.

Gloves

Have you ever tried pruning a rose without wearing gloves? At the very least, it is wise to wear a pair of sturdy gardening gloves to protect your hands (and forearms if the rose is a large shrub), as this is far better than dealing with the thorns and scratches. Strong leather gauntlets are a good start, but choose a pair with supple leather so that you can feel what you are doing when you are handling the plants.

The real danger comes when you start to use power tools for pruning and trimming, especially where the tools concerned are operating at high speed to cut through plant stems and branches. Always wear good-quality gloves when operating such machines.

Some plants, such as *Euphorbia* species (*see* above), exude sap that is very irritating to the skin. For trimming plants like this, a pair of rubber gloves will suffice.

Eye protection

All too often gardeners suffer from eye injuries. Most of these are caused by bending too close to the stubs of cut plants or canes (which have a very small 'profile' when viewed end on). Another risky time is when you are gathering up prunings, which often brings them close to your eyes. In these circumstances, eye protection in the form of goggles or safety glasses is worth considering.

With powered equipment, splinters or shards of stems and shoots can fly about in all directions, so you should always wear eye protection, regardless of whether your trimmer is powered by petrol or electricity. Also, when shredding prunings, the shredder may 'spit' small pieces of woody stem (especially from dry prunings) back out of the hopper.

Ear protection

Some sort of ear protection is essential when using powered pruning tools, so always wear earplugs or ear-defenders whenever possible. This is even more important if the machines are running for long periods. The best type of ear protection is something that muffles the noise rather than blocking it out completely. If you can't hear anything at all, if someone spots a hazard you have not seen you may not be able to hear their shouted warning. Petrol-driven tools and trimmers are particularly noisy.

Cable safety

With pruners and trimmers powered by mains electricity, the biggest drawback is the trailing cable. You spend most of your time wondering where it is and making sure you don't trip over it, cut through it or get it caught in some obstruction. Always try to have the cable positioned behind you, and well away from what you are cutting. You can buy gadgets that clip to your belt or clothing and hold an electric cable, while still allowing it to run freely but not impede movement while working.

Much of the health and safety emphasis is placed on avoiding cutting through a 'live' cable, and rightly so, but making sure that any cables are not going to wrap around feet or legs is every bit as important. Falling over while holding a power-driven trimmer or pruner (while it is running) is extremely dangerous.

Safety precautions

■ Tree-felling and the removal of large branches should be carried out by a profession tree surgeon. Never attempt to remove any tree over 5m (15ft) high.

■ When using a chainsaw, do so from the ground; for branches above waist height, always hire a tree surgeon.

■ Regular tetanus injections are advisable to eliminate the risk of infection from the tetanus bacterium, which is carried in soil and can enter through breaks in the skin. Adult boosters last for up to ten years, after which time they will have to be renewed.

■ Never trim plants in wet weather and wait until the plants themselves are dry.

■ Work from the ground wherever possible. Do not stretch out to reach growth while up a ladder.

■ Don't compost or shred diseased plant material, since it can infect other plants. Instead, burn it or dispose of it as waste.

Chainsaw safety

Chainsaws have the potential to be extremely dangerous, especially when the person using them has had no training. Ideally, it's best to employ a professional tree surgeon to do the work for you. However, if you do decide to hire a chainsaw, always insist on a demonstration and thorough instructions on how the machine works. If you are using one for the first time, make sure there is someone close by while you work, just in case things go wrong.

Don't forget

For any gardening equipment powered by mains electricity, always use an RCD (residual current device), also often referred to as a circuit breaker or trip switch. This device will make sure that the electricity supply to the cable stops instantaneously should you accidentally sever the power cable. If you have to use an extension cable, choose one with a brightly coloured outer casing that is easy to see – this greatly reduces the risk of cutting through it accidentally.

The chainsaw is probably the most dangerous of all pruning tools. Consider hiring a professional tree surgeon for major jobs.

Essential techniques

There is a wide selection of pruning tools to choose from (including your fingers!). The tool you select for a particular job will be determined by the reason for removal and the type of growth you are dealing with. Clean, precise cuts will heal better than rough and ragged ones, so all cutting blades should be kept clean and sharp.

Pruning with tools

Correct use of pruning tools is vital for your safety and the health of the plant. Using tools incorrectly can damage the plant and lead to infection and disease.

Using cutting tools

When using double-bladed cutting tools, such as secateurs, loppers and pole pruners, never twist or lever the blades to try to speed up the cutting process. This will only strain the pivotal nut that holds the blades in place; once this has been damaged, the blades will be misaligned and unable to make clean cuts. If you find you are having to twist or lever, it means you are using the wrong tool for the job.

When you position the blades for cutting, make sure the stem is centrally placed between the tips and the pivotal point of the blades, erring on the side of the pivotal point. This will give you the firmest possible grip on the stem. Making cuts with the tips of the blades is likely to strain or force them apart.

When using a pruning saw, always cut a branch off close to a trunk or main stem. Don't leave a stump that will die back and don't cut flush to the stem. If you leave a 'collar' at the base of the branch (*see* box, opposite) it will encourage

bark to grow over the wound and will heal better.

Use a gardening knife to smooth the rough edges of pruning cuts to prevent infection.

Where to cut

The position of a pruning cut on the stem or branch of a plant is very important as it can have a direct bearing on how well (and how quickly) a cut may heal – and in some cases whether a cut can heal at all. It also affects how quickly the plant responds to the cut – that is,

When using double-bladed tools, such as loppers (above) or secateurs, cut near the pivotal point of the blades rather than the tips.

Where and how to make a cut

For plants that have buds arranged alternately on the stem (below left), make a diagonal cut just above a bud. The cut should slope down behind the bud. Ideally, the cut will be at an angle of about 25 degrees. Where a plant has opposite buds (below right), and an angled cut is difficult, make a horizontal cut straight across the stem, just above a pair of buds. In both cases, cut about 6mm (¼in) above the bud.

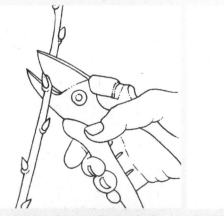

Pruning above an alternate bud **Pruning above a pair of opposite buds**

how quickly new growth will spring from the pruned section.

A plant's growth hormones are concentrated in the area of the buds. As well as encouraging growth, these hormones promote healing. So it makes sense to make your cuts close to a live bud (though not so close that you risk damaging it). As a general rule, the ideal place to cut is 6mm (¼in) above the bud. (The only time you might not want to cut close to a bud is when you are trying to discourage growth, such as when you completely cut out unwanted stems.) Remember that the direction in which the bud points is an indication of the direction that the new growth will take once the stem is pruned. So if you want new growth to spring to the right, don't cut above a bud that is pointing to the left.

How to cut

Wherever possible, stems should be cut at a slight angle to encourage sap or rainwater to drain off rather than accumulate on the cut surface (where it will inhibit the healing process). Note that the angle should be slight (say, 25 degrees); if it is greater than this, you negate much of the benefit of making the angled cut because you increase the surface area of the cut – the greater the surface area the greater the area of entry for harmful bacteria or viruses.

The buds on most plants are arranged either alternately or in opposite pairs on the stem. For plants with alternate buds, it is easy to make the angled cut (the cut should slope down from the bud). For plants with opposite buds, there is no alternative but to cut straight across, just above the pair of buds, as shown opposite.

Removing large branches

It is often difficult to estimate the size and weight of a branch, and they always seem to be larger and heavier than you think – especially if they are removed or reduced in the summer, when they are full of sap. For very large branches, it is safer to hire a professional tree surgeon to carry out the work. If you are removing a large branch yourself, it is always best to remove it in stages, rather than try to cut it off all in one go, to avoid the branch ripping away and damaging the tree trunk.

Make the first cut *underneath* the branch being removed (*see* below left), about 30–45cm (12–18in) away from the trunk. The cut should slice about a quarter of the way through the branch. Make a deeper cut in the top of the branch, a few centimetres away from the first. The bulk of the branch should then fall gently away, leaving a stump.

To remove the stub (*see* below right), make a third cut close to the trunk. Take care to leave the collar (ridge of bark where the branch joins the trunk), as this will help the wound to heal and reduce the chances of infection. Wound-sealant paint is available, but research shows this may do more harm than good (*see* box, page 31).

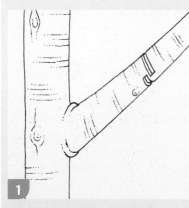

1 Make two cuts in the branch: one beneath, the other in the top.

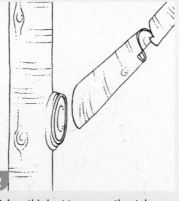

2 Make a third cut to remove the stub, leaving a 'collar' on the tree.

The large branch on the right-hand side of this *Robinia pseudoacacia* 'Frisia' is likely to break off if its weight is not reduced by pruning. It is best to remove large branches in stages (*see* box, left).

Hand-pruning techniques

Soft shoots, dead flowers and suckers (*see* page 33) are often more easily removed by hand than with pruning tools.

Dead-heading

Dead-heading (the removal of dead flowers) is one of the simplest forms of pruning. It involves removing any old, spent flowers in order to prevent seeds forming. It is a way of 'fooling' the plant into thinking it hasn't yet reproduced, and as a result it will often prolong flowering. To dead-head a plant, pluck off any dead blooms when they start to fade and turn brown. The way in which you do this depends on the type of flower you are dealing with, and whether it has long or short stems. In the case of thicker, woodier stems, for example those of roses, you will need to use secateurs (*see* page 87).

If you are dead-heading long-stemmed plants, such as pelargoniums, remove the stalk as well as the dead flower. Break it off cleanly at the point where it grows out from the main stem of the plant.

Finger pruning

This technique (sometimes known as 'pinch pruning') involves using your fingers rather than tools to prune. It is used to remove soft young growth of some plants, such as fuchsias and penstemons. You can use either the fingernails of your thumb and fore-finger to pull out the sideshoots, or if they're small, rub them out with the side of your finger.

Stopping One of the aims of finger pruning is to make young plants branch and form an attractive bushy shape. Many plants have a natural tendency to grow upwards, becoming tall and lanky rather than filling out nicely. This is known as 'apical dominance' (*see* page 13). Plants whose stems display apical dominance have natural hormones that encourage the bud at the stem tip to keep growing so that the stem gets longer and longer. However, if the gardener nips out the tip at the end of the stem, the hormones are deflected to the next buds down, which are then triggered into growth to produce sideshoots. This pruning technique is often

With short-stemmed flowers, such as camellias, nip the dead heads off with your fingers just behind the flower.

known as 'stopping', as a plant's natural growth habit is checked. It is best carried out when potting up rooted cuttings.

Pinching out The same technique is also used on mature plants with soft growth, to maintain a neat habit. For instance, the plant may be growing in a lopsided way and you'll want to create a more balanced shape by removing over-long shoots. You should also remove shoots that have been damaged by frost or pests and diseases. Removing the damaged shoot gets rid of the unsightly plant part as well as any unwanted pests present, and it acts as a trigger to the plant to produce a new shoot. This technique of removing growing shoots on mature plants is sometimes known as 'pinching out'.

Keeping pruned plants healthy

Pruning is generally beneficial for plants, but in some cases it can take its toll. The removal of leafy shoots can deprive the plant of its source of energy, and stimulating more vigorous flowering or fruiting will put further demands on the plant. In addition, pruning can leave a plant vulnerable to infection or other damage, such as excessive 'bleeding'. But don't be put off by all this – if you follow a few simple rules you should be able to avoid problems before they arise.

An annual mulch of organic matter, such as garden compost (above) or horse manure, will keep plants healthy and, combined with fertilizer, will help to reduce the chance of infections taking hold after pruning.

Feeding and mulching

Pruning can check a plant's growth potential, especially if pruned while it is actively growing. For this reason, to get the best results, feed plants soon after they have been pruned. Most plants pruned between spring and midsummer need a general fertilizer that contains a balanced combination of nutrients, including nitrogen, phosphates and potassium, together with essential trace elements. However, in some cases you may need to use a different type of fertilizer. For example, if you were pruning a hedge in spring you would feed it with a fertilizer that contains high levels of nitrogen to promote new growth; pruning the same hedge in late summer and feeding it with a fertilizer that is higher in phosphates and potash will encourage the production of slower, harder growth that can withstand the winter cold much better.

If you're undertaking a major renovation programme of a neglected plant (see pages 17–18), feeding is particularly important, as you will be putting more strain on the plant. Remember, it is better to apply several small feeds rather than one large one, as this will help to provide steady new growth rather

than very soft, sappy shoots that are susceptible to pests and diseases.

After you've applied fertilizer, it's a good idea to apply a mulch, such as well-rotted farmyard manure or garden compost. Mulching provides low levels of valuable plant nutrients, it helps to keep the plant's roots at an even temperature and retains moisture in the soil. If the mulch is deep enough (ideally 8–10cm/3–4in deep) it will also suppress weeds that would compete with the plants for water, nutrients and (if they grow tall enough) light.

Preventing infection

Every time you saw off a branch, or cut a root or shoot with a knife or secateurs, there is always a chance that the wound you have made can become infected. Until the cut surface has hardened and dried, the wound is open to fungal and bacterial rots entering the plant. If undetected or left untreated, the infection may lead to the eventual death of the plant.

It is worth remembering that healthy, vigorous, well-fed plants are much more able to fight off infection naturally than poor, weak, sickly plants ever could. The speed at which a pruning wound heals is always a good indication of how

healthy a plant is; rapid healing of a cut is a sure sign that a plant is healthy and growing well.

Timing

One way to reduce the chance of infection is to prune during the summer, when wound healing takes place more rapidly and there are far

Natural healing process

Traditionally, gardeners used wound paint to cover a pruning wound. These used to contain fungicides or tar extract, but these toxic substances have been phased out in favour of treatments containing natural plant resins. However, extensive research has now shown that there is really no benefit to be gained from using any type of wound paint. Indeed, these treatments may actually seal fungal spores into the cut and aid infection rather than healing. This has led to a trend away from using wound treatments and towards encouraging the plant's natural immune system to heal the wounds.

fewer fungal spores drifting in the air to land on cut surfaces and open wounds. Many *Prunus* species (members of the cherry family) are pruned at this time to reduce the risk of infection by silver leaf fungus, which is a common cause of death in these plants. *Acer* species (Japanese maples) are often pruned while they are actively growing to counter possible infection from coral spot fungus, which frequently invades live growth after establishing itself on dead twigs.

The timing of pruning in relation to the growth cycle of the plant is also important. For example, broad-leaved evergreens and conifers tend to have two surges of growth each year, one in spring and one in late summer or early autumn; so, for the most rapid healing of pruning cuts, you should prune just before these growth surges.

Techniques and tools

The rapid healing of pruning cuts is closely linked to making good, clean pruning cuts using the correct technique (*see* pages 28–9). Generally, you should make as many cuts as possible close to a branch join or fork, often referred to as the 'branch bark ridge', which is the slight swelling at the point where a branch joins another branch or the main trunk of the plant. This is the most important area, as it is where an open wound will heal most rapidly and where the naturally occurring chemical and physical barriers within the wood that offer resistance to the invasion of rot-causing fungi are found. So, by pruning at this point, the plant's own natural 'immune system' has the best possible chance of protecting it against the invasion of fungal decay.

Like the other species of maple, *Acer shirasawanum* 'Aureum' is one of the plants that are especially prone to coral spot disease and 'bleeding'. It is therefore best pruned in the summer.

To help pruning cuts heal quickly, it is essential that all cutting implements, such as saws, knives, loppers and secateurs, are clean and sharp. Clean, precise, carefully positioned cuts will always heal more quickly than rough-edged cuts with bruised woody tissue and torn or jagged bark.

Dieback

Sometimes a shoot or branch starts to turn brown and die off from the tip downwards. This is called 'dieback' and is caused by disease. Any affected shoots should be cut out as soon as you see them. Prune well below the dead area so that the disease cannot infect the rest of the plant.

Preventing 'bleeding'

Another type of pruning damage can occur in those plants that are prone to excessive sap loss – known as 'bleeding' – through the cut surfaces. Some plants can lose a lot of their strength and vigour if they are allowed to bleed sap for long periods, and this will slow down the sealing and healing process on the newly cut surface, so the wound remains vulnerable to infection. To make matters worse, where bleeding occurs the section of stem immediately beneath the pruning cut may start to die back away from the wounded area, leaving bare dead stumps or sections of branch that will need to be pruned out later.

One way to overcome these problems is to prune plants that are at risk – namely, *Acer* (maple), *Aesculus* (horse chestnut), *Betula* (birch), *Vitis* species (vines) and *Juglans* (walnut) – in mid- to late summer, when they are in full leaf, rather than in winter or spring.

The leaves will draw up water, which then evaporates from the leaf surface (a process called 'transpiration'). Because the pull of the leaves is so strong, much of the sap is drawn past the open wounds, allowing them to start healing more quickly.

Removing suckers

Many trees and shrubs have a suckering habit, which means that they produce new shoots, or 'suckers', from their roots; some other plants may produce suckers after they have been pruned hard or if they have been damaged.

Suckers may spread out from the roots around the plant you have pruned, or they may grow from the stem or trunk of the plant, either at or just above ground level. Most suckers do not actually damage the plant, but they may sap its energy. However, if the plant concerned has been propagated onto a rootstock – for instance in the case of a rose (*see* page 89) – the problem is more severe, because the unwanted, more vigorous shoots of the stock plant will eventually take over and replace the grafted cultivar.

All suckers should be removed as soon as you see them. Where plants produce sucker growths from a rootstock, try to rip or pull them from the plant at the point of origin, rather than cutting them off. If you cut them off, some dormant buds are more likely to remain at the base of the shoot to produce new suckers. If the suckers have formed a clump some distance from the plant, pull or dig them out with a spade.

(*see* page 89)

Plants prone to suckering

Ailanthus
Aralia elata and cultivars
Celastrus
Clerodendrum
Corylus avellana 'Contorta'
Embothrium
Fallopia aubertii, *F. baldschuanica*
Gleditsia
Hippophae
Kerria japonica
Malus (fruiting and ornamental)
Populus
Prunus (fruiting and ornamental)
Pyrus (fruiting and ornamental)
Rhus typhina
Robinia
Rosa (species and shrubs)
Syringa cultivars
Tilia
Wisteria

Rhus typhina is a wonderful small tree with elegant, fern-like foliage. However, it suckers profusely and the shoots can appear some distance from the plant. Be careful where you plant it and remove suckers as they appear.

Pruning garden plants

There are dozens of reasons for pruning all the different kinds of plants; from trees and shrubs to roses and climbers. In addition to pruning for the plant's sake – its health and vigour – you might want to encourage an attractive shape in a young tree, get loads of good fruit from your bushes, persuade a climber to drape itself over a pergola, or adorn a hedge with topiary shapes. This section explains how to prune all these various types of plants and – essentially – shows you how to get them doing what you want them to do and not whatever they please.

Trees

Trees come in all shapes and sizes. The reason for this is not just natural habit, as with weeping trees or columnar conifers, in a surprising number of cases a tree is the shape and size it is because someone armed with a set of pruning tools has intervened. There are a number of methods for pruning trees, each designed for a particular purpose, but the first thing you need to know is when to prune (and when not to).

When to prune trees

Most deciduous trees are pruned when they are dormant, usually in late autumn and through winter. They have their main surge of growth from spring until early summer. Broad-leaved evergreens, such as box or holly, tend to have their main growing period at the same time of year, but will often have an additional, smaller surge of growth in late summer. Conifers have two distinct surges of growth: one in late spring and early summer, and another in late summer and early autumn. As a general rule, if you prune just before these surges of growth (especially before the spring surge), you will see the most rapid and positive results and speedy healing of any wounds.

Of course, with any rules there are exceptions, and for practical reasons (usually the protection of the plant) certain trees need to be pruned at other times of year. Some trees grown mainly for their flowers are best pruned soon after their period of flowering (*see* pages 38–9) – there are various reasons for this, but in

many cases it is to ensure flowers for the following year. Also, *Acer* (maple), *Betula* (birch) and *Juglans* (walnut) will 'bleed' excess amounts of sap if they are pruned in late winter or early spring, so they are often pruned in late summer, while they are in full leaf. This is because moisture in the stems is drawn up into the leaves and tends to bypass the pruning cuts, reducing any 'bleeding'. Cherries are often summer pruned to reduce the chances of contracting the fatal disease silver leaf, of which there are fewer spores in summer.

Birches (here, *Betula utilis* var. *jacquemontii*) should be pruned only when dormant, between late summer and midwinter, to prevent 'bleeding'.

Pruning of ornamental cherries (here, *Prunus* 'Shirotae') should be kept to a minimum; if it is necessary, prune in midsummer and keep cuts small.

Raising young trees

With most trees, pruning in the early stages of life (known as formative pruning) really gives them a good headstart. A balanced crown with evenly spaced branches and wide branch angles will have few problems as it ages, unlike one that has had no formative pruning.

A tree that has been allowed to develop potential faults while young may prove problematic as it matures, with narrow forks causing splitting and cavities forming as a result, while a misshapen or unbalanced crown may affect the tree's stability as it gets larger and the branches become heavier. The method of pruning most tree types is very similar in the first two growing seasons. After this, specific training into the various tree forms begins. (Although if you buy a ready-trained young tree this stage will have been started off for you.)

With all newly planted trees it's vital to encourage them to establish a good, spreading root system. This usually involves staking the tree when it is planted. This extra support will keep the root system stable so that new roots can grow into the surrounding soil, but the top of the tree can move in the wind so that the stem and branches thicken up naturally. Regardless of the time of year, if any damaged roots or shoots are seen during planting they should be trimmed straight away.

Creating a standard

Most garden trees tend to be grown as standards, with a single trunk cleared of any lower branches. Standards are the most popular form of tree because they fit well into a garden setting – their clear stems allow light into the centre of the tree and provide space underneath their canopy so that shrubs, lawn grasses and other plants are able to grow relatively close to the tree's base. For most young trees, this is not a natural habit of growth – in fact, if left to their own devices it is very rare for a tree to form a clear stem until it reaches maturity (which may be anything from 25 to 150 years, depending on the tree's life span).

To achieve a clear stem the gardener needs to remove the lower branches when the tree is young. This has to be done in stages by

HOW TO create a standard from a young tree

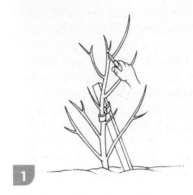

1 In the first winter after planting, remove any shoots that are competing with the main stem, and cut out shoots that are crossing over one another. If these rub against each other a wound can develop, which can let in fungal spores.

2 During the following spring, remove all of the shoots from the lower third of the stem, cutting them back close to the main stem. On the middle third of the stem, reduce all the shoots by half their length to encourage the main stem to thicken.

3 In the second winter, cut off those shoots that had been reduced by half close to the main stem, to leave another section clear of branches.

4 As the new growth starts in spring, cut back the branches on the next section by half, and trim back any shoots that are competing with the growing tip of the main stem.

Young acers (here, *A. carpinifolium*) can be encouraged to branch low to show off their attractive leaves, or if they have decorative bark they are usually grown with clear trunks.

gradually reducing the length of the branches before removing them altogether (*see* opposite).

This process is carried out to allow the tree stem to thicken naturally so that it is strong enough to support the 'head' of branches. Removing these branches before they become too thick also prevents any possibility of creating large wounds and scars along the tree trunk later on.

Nursery-bought trees are often trained as standards already.

Pruning established trees

Once most trees have established (and if the formative pruning was effective), there should be little need for a set maintenance-pruning programme. However, dying, dead or damaged parts should be removed as soon as they are spotted to prevent diseases from taking hold. In spring and summer, cut off any shoots growing on the clear stem of standard trees, and remove suckers from around the tree as soon as they emerge (*see* page 33).

Although in most cases it is advisable to carry out moderate pruning during the dormant season (there are a few exceptions, *see* page 35), it's best to avoid severe pruning at this time. Pruning tends to provoke growth, and heavy pruning of dormant plants frequently leads to the production of large numbers of thin, weak, sappy 'water shoots' (also known as epicormic shoots), which grow through the centre of the tree and on the stubs of stems that have been pruned. These water shoots, especially those in the centre of the crown, will need to be cut out again or they will cause congestion in the centre of the tree. This can lead to fungal diseases taking hold because the air circulation through the branches is reduced. They will also divert energy from the rest of the tree. Cut out either whole branches or sections of branch and create space for new stems to develop and grow into these spaces (*see* How to prune a standard flowering tree, page 38).

Improving balance and form

Some trees will naturally form an unbalanced crown, where one or more limbs grow more vigorously than neighbouring ones. If they are left unchecked their weight and length may cause the tree to lean and become unstable, so some pruning may be needed to maintain the crown's shape and balance.

Some trees, for instance *Betula* (birch), have a strong tendency to produce shoots that compete with the central leader or main stem of the tree; if these competing leaders are allowed to develop, the main stem will eventually fork. This makes the tree very prone to wind damage, particularly the risk of the stem splitting as the tree gets older and these limbs become much heavier. The sooner you deal with vigorous side branches or competing leaders, the lower the likelihood of faults developing. That said, birches look particularly attractive when grown as multi-stemmed plants from an early age (*see* below).

Betula (birch) species can be grown as multi-stemmed trees to maximize their bark appeal.

Flowering trees

Trees that are principally grown for their flowers should, ideally, be pruned according to the time of year at which they normally bloom.

With trees such as *Malus* (crab apple), *Prunus* (ornamental cherry) and *Pyrus* (ornamental pear), which produce their flowers on the previous season's growth, the ideal time to prune is just after they have finished flowering. This gives the tree time to produce the new shoots that will become next year's flowering growth. Winter-flowering trees should also be pruned soon after flowering, as any cuts should heal quickly if the tree is healthy because it will be going through its most rapid phase of growth. Trees that flower up until midsummer can be pruned as soon as the petals fall, while those that flower in late summer and autumn are pruned when they are dormant. With flowering trees that also produce ornamental fruits (*see* opposite), the difficulty is knowing when to prune to get the best of both worlds – flowers and fruits.

Like other ornamental trees, you can renewal prune flowering trees in winter, but doing too much pruning at this time of year can be counterproductive. Many flowering trees bloom in spring, so there is a risk that doing anything other than essential structural pruning will result in the removal of stems that should be flowering within a few months.

The time may come, as with this old apple tree, when little pruning is needed and the tree's natural habit is acceptable.

HOW TO prune a standard flowering tree

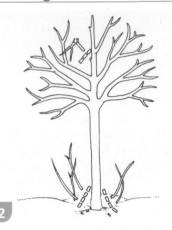

1 In winter, remove any thin, whippy water shoots (*see* page 37) from the centre of the tree and thin out overcrowded shoots. This will prevent congestion and keep the remaining shoots growing strongly. Reduce the length of any vigorous shoots that spoil the overall shape or balance of the crown.

2 In spring and summer (after flowering), cut out any dead, dying or damaged shoots, prune any shoots growing on the clear stem of standard trees, and remove suckers from around the tree as soon as they emerge. Branches, or sections of branches, can be removed to allow room for replacement shoots to grow.

Some trees, such as this *Sorbus commixta*, are grown for their beautiful clusters of berries. To ensure that these are not compromised, these trees should be pruned only when they are dormant.

Trees with decorative fruits

Trees like *Sorbus* (mountain ash, rowan and whitebeam) are prized more for their attractive autumn berry colour than for their flowers. You can prune these either when they are dormant (although this may lead to some flower-bearing wood being removed) or just after flowering to remove overlapping branches and reduce overcrowding. The aim is to retain a balanced crown with no competing leaders or branches with narrow angles, which may lead to splitting later.

Pollarded trees have a permanent stem and a temporary canopy – it is replaced every one or two years as a result of hard pruning the top of the stem.

Pollarding

Some trees respond to regular hard pruning (or pollarding) of the top growth by producing vigorous new branches that are of ornamental value. Pollarding produces wonderful results in trees whose primary attraction is their brightly coloured young stems or leaves – the crown consists only of striking, juvenile growth and is renewed regularly. Pollarding may also be used to restrict a tree's size where space is limited. Only a small number of trees can tolerate such hard pruning, including *Salix* (willow) which is often pollarded for its bright ornamental stems, *Tilia* (lime), *Ailanthus* (tree of heaven), *Catalpa bignonioides* (Indian bean tree), *Platanus × hispanica* (plane), *Castanea sativa* (sweet chestnut), *Cercis* (Judas tree) and *Morus alba* (white mulberry).

How to pollard a tree

A tree intended for pollarding is initially grown as a standard, with a 'leg' or stem cleared of any lower branches. With the likes of willow and mulberry you can take a shortcut. Cut a 2–3m (6–10ft) long, one-year-old shoot from an existing plant and stick this into the ground where you intend it to grow so that you have a ready-made standard stem. When the tree has grown, cut the top off the plant 1.5–2m (5–6ft) above ground level.

In winter, while the plant is dormant, cut back to about 5cm (2in) long all the thick, strong shoots that will have sprouted from

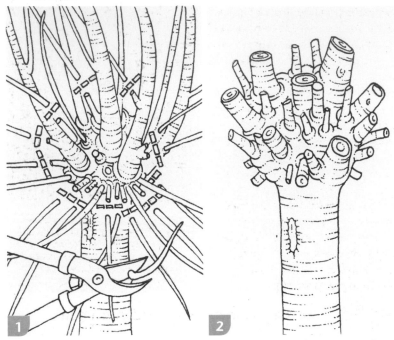

1 In winter, cut back hard all the shoots that have sprouted from the top of the plant's stem.

2 From these stubs fresh young growths will emerge, carrying bright green shoots and effectively renewing the canopy.

the top of the stem. Remove any thin, weak shoots. In summer, cut out any thin, weak shoots and any that are dying back; also remove any growths that emerge on the main stem below the crown of the tree.

Severe annual pruning can put a great strain on a tree and make it vulnerable to attack from pests and diseases, so it is better for the plant if it is pollarded in alternate years.

Don't forget

Pollarding can save trees that have become too big for their situation, but pollarding of large, established trees must be carried out only by a professional tree surgeon.

Coppicing or stooling

Coppicing involves the regular (sometimes annual) cutting back of a tree (or shrub, *see* page 53) to ground level, to restrict size or for ornamental reasons. Some trees (such as *Eucalyptus* or *Paulownia*) tend to grow to a great height and become totally out of scale with the rest of the garden. In this situation it can be a disastrous mistake to remove the top of the tree, as the shape becomes totally distorted. It is better to cut the whole tree down to about 15cm (6in) above ground level in spring. Then, as new shoots emerge from around the stump, leave one to form a replacement stem and remove all the others while they are still small. Although it seems drastic, this type of pruning can be used every three or four years to prevent the tree becoming too large.

Alternatively, you can use coppicing to make the tree form a clump of stems rather than a trunk (a bit like a 'legless' pollarded tree). This can be particularly useful for creating hedges – *Carpinus betulus* (hornbeam), *Corylus* (hazel), *Fagus sylvatica* (beech) and *Taxus baccata* (yew) can all be coppiced to create multi-stemmed plants suitable for hedging. Once you've cut the tree down, allow four or five shoots to grow and form the multi-stemmed clump. To keep it this way you will need to continue coppicing every year or two.

Coppicing may seem drastic, but it is a good way to control the size of vigorous trees that would otherwise outgrow their allotted space.

Evergreen trees

In general, evergreen trees should be pruned between late summer and early winter. They divide into two main pruning groups: broad-leaved evergreens (including hollies, box, magnolias and camellias – although the latter are trained as shrubs in their early years) and conifers.

Broad-leaved evergreens

These usually need little maintenance pruning, especially if they are pruned and shaped well when they are young. They always do better if the main stem or central leader is retained rather than pruned out; this will keep the plant growing upwards until you decide it has reached the height you would like it to be. Most of your pruning should be aimed at encouraging the side stems to divide into branches. This way, you encourage strong, bushy growth rather than long, lax stems. You also need to remove the tips of any shoots that compete with the main stem and try to change the direction of growth.

Check trees regularly and remove any dead or diseased shoots. In spring, trim back any frost-damaged shoot tips as soon as you see them. Those forms of box or holly that have brightly coloured, variegated leaves may need extra pruning to remove any green shoots that have reverted. If this is not done, the more vigorous green shoots will eventually swamp the variegated growth in a process known as 'reversion' (*see* page 15).

With variegated evergreens, such as this holly, keep a sharp eye out for any signs of reversion. Shoots that come through green rather than variegated should be pruned out immediately.

Camellias, like other broad-leaved evergreens, need little maintenance pruning once they have matured.

HOW TO prune a young broad-leaved evergreen

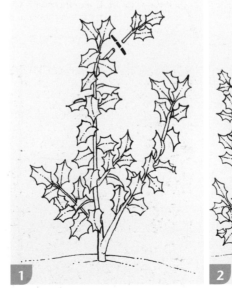

1 After planting the tree, remove the tips of any shoots that compete with the leader. The aim is to form a straight, single-stemmed tree with sideshoots close to ground level.

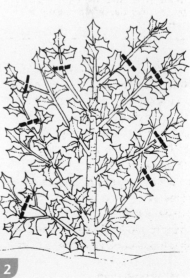

2 In spring, trim back any shoot tips as necessary to help the plant become more bushy, and remove any green, reverted shoots on variegated plants (very important on holly).

The aim of training is to create a very productive tree growing in a confined space in its own 'microclimate'. The tree is usually grown against a support structure and is regularly pruned and tied in to achieve a particular shape. The microclimate protects more frost-tender plants, or encourages hardier ones to flower and fruit slightly earlier than normal.

Fan

This shape is often used for plants grown against a wall or fence, particularly ones that need shelter or warmth. Although the pruning and training method is quite intensive, when done well these plants can be attractive in winter – even when they are just a framework of bare shoots.

When the tree is young, the main stem is pruned to encourage a branching habit. The resulting sideshoots ('laterals') are pruned, trained and tied in to create an evenly spaced framework of branches that go on to produce flower- or fruit-bearing shoots. The shoots may be tied to canes as they grow and are gradually moved into position over several months to make sure the support surface is evenly covered with tiered shoots, all with a similar amount of growing space.

For most plants, pruning in both spring and summer will be necessary to maintain the shape of the fan. This will also help to maximize the growth potential of the tree.

Cordon

A cordon consists of one or more main stems, which form the main framework of the tree or shrub, and side branches trained to form fruit-bearing spurs. Many single-stemmed cordon apple trees are grown as 'oblique' cordons, planted and trained at an angle of 45 degrees, to restrict the natural vigour of the plants and to encourage more fruit production.

Redcurrants and gooseberry plants can also be trained as cordons, but these are usually grown as upright stems, often with two or more stems (apples can also be cultivated as multi-stemmed upright cordons). The problem with this method is trying to balance the growth evenly between the number of stems involved.

Like fans, cordons will need pruning at least twice a year – once while they are growing and once while dormant. They will also need regular tying in and

These are all space-saving ways of growing trees. They are highly ornamental and, in many cases, improve flowering or fruiting.
① A fan-trained morello cherry.
② A line of cordon-grown apples.
③ A pear trained as an espalier.
④ An olive tree grown as a standard.

training to direct the growth into the desired shape and direction. The main advantage of training plants like this is that heavy crops of fruit can be produced in a relatively small area.

Espalier

This is possibly the most difficult type of training. The aim is to create several tiers of perfectly symmetrical branches, evenly spaced along a single, vertical main stem. A very strong support system of horizontal wires running along a wall or fence, or between stout posts, is essential. Although this shape is most commonly associated with apples and pears, pyracanthas grown as wall shrubs also work well as espaliers.

The tiers of branches are formed by cutting the growing tip out of the main stem to create a minimum of three new shoots: one to grow upwards to act as a replacement for the main stem, and at least two others to be trained out in opposite directions horizontally. This process is repeated each year until the desired number of tiers is formed. As with other methods of training, the shoots are pruned and tied to canes before they can be bent down into a horizontal position. This is the tricky bit, because the tree is being forced to grow against its natural habit.

Both summer and winter pruning are needed, with the lateral shoots being trimmed to form fruiting spurs along the entire length of the horizontal branches.

Standard

Standard trees have a clear stem (with no branches) and a crown or 'head' of branches on the top. There are two types: 'natural' and 'grafted' standards.

Natural standard The framework of branches that forms the head of a tree will develop naturally on the extension of the main stem, known as the 'central leader', which continues to grow upwards as the tree ages. With weeping standards, the head is made of lax, weeping branches formed above the clear stem or 'leg', often with the branches trailing down almost to the ground.

Grafted standard A plant with a vigorous rootstock is grown to form a single upright stem or 'leg', with the side branches being cleared from the stem in stages over two, three or four years, depending on the plant. Once this stem has reached a height of 1.5–2m (5–6ft), the top is cut off and another plant (usually a cultivar chosen for its decorative qualities) is grafted onto the top. If the graft is successful, a new head forms, which may be upright or weeping in habit. Weeping forms of ash, birch, beech, pussy willow and cherry (as well as upright types of cherry) are often sold as grafted standards.

Conifers

It's important to prune conifers between autumn and early winter, not before. Conifers start into active growth in early spring, often with a second flush in late summer and early autumn, so avoid pruning at these times as some conifers 'bleed' sap copiously when in active growth.

Tree-like conifers (as opposed to ground-cover and shrubby ones) tend to develop a single main stem or leader, with branches radiating

Conifers form a highly diverse group of evergreen trees, with habits varying from broadly conical to narrowly columnar. Pruning will help to develop these upright shapes.

The Monterey pine (here, *Pinus radiata* 'Marshwood'), with its bright green foliage, is narrow and conical when young, becoming broader with age.

around the stem, often in clearly defined layers, creating the typical conifer shape. The growing point and new growth immediately around it can look very thin and straggly in the tree's early years, but as the tree ages this growth will change to resemble the lower parts of the plant.

Formative pruning As soon as they are spotted, any upright branches that appear to compete

with the leading shoot should be shortened to allow the original lead shoot to dominate the direction of growth (*see* below). It may benefit the plant if this lead shoot is supported with a cane to keep it upright. Any trimming of the lower side branches is usually limited to shortening those shoots that are over-vigorous and spoiling the overall shape and balance of the young plant.

Mature conifers Most mature conifers are best grown with minimal pruning. However, you do need to remove dead, dying or damaged wood. Usually this is easily seen, since it tends to become very discoloured and eventually brown. At the same time, you can also trim back any shoots that are growing very vigorously and spoiling the balance and shape of the plant.

Juniperus squamata cultivars (here, 'Blue Carpet'), may be grown as shrubs for their bushy or spreading habit, or as small upright trees.

After planting, or in the first spring after planting, remove the tips of any shoots that are competing with the leader. Trim back any shoot tips as necessary to help the plant become more bushy.

With many conifers, do try to avoid cutting into the old wood as it is very rare for a conifer to produce new, green growth from old (brown) wood. Although the plant may still be alive, no shoots will develop from the bare areas. The dense growth of many conifers at their branch tips produces a dead 'interior': between the branch tips and the main stem, twigs and buds die from lack of light. This 'dead zone' limits the extent of pruning, because if it is exposed new leaves and shoots will not develop from that area and it will look unsightly. Always cut into green growth so that the plant can regenerate.

Large, mature conifers with an upright habit do not respond well to having their tops removed. This 'topping' removes the most actively growing portion of the crown of the tree. The result is that the tree becomes misshapen, with the top tier of branches all trying to replace the lead shoot, giving a table-top appearance that spoils the profile of the tree.

With pines and spruces, the buds that produce the new shoots each year are found only on the tips of the older shoots and are most visible in spring. Because of their appearance, these shoots are sometimes referred to as 'candles'. In order to encourage a plant to branch more, wait until the candle has grown almost to its full length and the needles are still soft, and then cut the candle back by around half its length.

Renovation and restructuring

A tree that has been neglected, or allowed to outgrow its position, need not be removed; if it is healthy and stable, most problems can be rectified. However, a tree that is dangerous because it is fundamentally unstable is always better replaced.

As with any form of drastic pruning, major renovation or restructuring work will put the tree under stress. The best approach is to do it in stages; if you stagger the work over two or three years, you will give the tree a better chance of surviving the processs. You can renovate a tree at any time of year, except in spring when growth begins. Trees that produce sap, such as birches (*Betula*) should be pruned in

late autumn or winter for best results.

The first stage of any renovation or restructuring work is to remove dead, damaged or diseased wood. After this, you can begin pruning to achieve your purpose. You can give it a bit of a haircut to tidy up the overall shape; or you can thin it out – to improve light into (or views out of) your garden or to reduce the amount of shade it casts; or you can lift the crown – remove lower branches – to improve access beneath the canopy.

Crown reduction

This is done to reduce a tree's size without affecting overall shape and balance. With small trees, it can be attempted by the amateur; with larger trees it is better left to a tree surgeon because it can be difficult to get to the ends of the branches without mishap, and it's not that easy to prune all branches evenly to preserve symmetry.

Crown thinning

This is the removal of excess branches throughout the canopy to allow more light to pass through. It also improves stability because it reduces the tree's resistance to wind. Since the limbs being removed are near the trunk, the actual pruning is easier than for crown reduction. However, thinning a crown without upsetting overall balance and symmetry takes quite a bit of skill and practice, so it can be difficult for the amateur to get it right.

Crown lifting

This involves reducing the depth of the crown by removing the lower branches – to facilitate access or to enable you to create a seating area beneath it. It is the easiest tree surgery technique to master, as identifying which branches to remove and where to cut is straightforward, and you may not even have to leave the ground to do it. However, do check to see if any upright branches are growing from the branches you want to cut off as their removal may affect the overall shape of the crown. When you have decided which branches to cut, prune them back to the main trunk (*see* page 29).

Crown reduction (far left) is the short back and sides of tree surgery. Crown thinning (left, middle) involves removing branches to reduce the density of the canopy. Crown lifting (left) is the removal of the lower branches. The method you use will depend on your purpose and the finished effect you are trying to achieve.

Shrubs

This large group of woody plants causes the most problems when it comes to pruning. There are so many different types, with a wide variety of habits and pruning requirements, that it is all too easy to lose confidence or abandon the idea of pruning them altogether. Most shrubs, however, will definitely perform better (and usually live longer) if they are pruned regularly, so if you can get to grips with the principles, it's worth having a go.

Hamamelis × intermedia 'Diane' wafts a heady scent through the winter garden and is a shrub that requires little or no pruning.

A number of very good shrubs hardly ever seem to need any pruning other than to dead-head the old flowers, prune out any dead or damaged shoots, or trim the growth lightly to keep the shape balanced. Others, if left to their own devices, will gradually become unattractive and deteriorate over time as the growth suffers and the health and vigour declines. Indeed, the amount you prune and the pruning method you use can have a major effect on the lifespan of a shrub. A complete lack of pruning or, conversely, frequent severe pruning often result in the plant living for a shorter period than one pruned on a regular basis.

Different pruning methods are needed to maintain evergreen shrubs, or those grown for their flowers, winter stems or autumn colour (such as these *Cornus*, *Sorbus* and *Berberis*).

Reasons for pruning

Just how and why a shrub is pruned will depend on the type of shrub, the stage of development of the plant concerned and how healthy and vigorous the plant is at the time. It is also very important to consider what a plant is being used for and what you wish to achieve, as the same type of plant may be pruned in different ways to produce different effects. Many shrubs are best pruned soon after flowering, especially if you are not sure what they are or when to prune. However, this may cost a plant such as *Callicarpa bodinieri* its attractive fruits in autumn/winter, so pruning should be delayed until the wild birds have removed the berries.

Formative pruning

This type of pruning is used for young and recently planted shrubs or those that have been cut back to renovate and reinvigorate them. The aim is to develop a sound structural framework for the future, with well-developed, evenly spaced branches and stems. At this stage of the plant's life, you are not aiming for flowers or ornamental fruits. Where possible, always try to work with the plant and follow its natural growth pattern.

The amount of pruning a plant requires at this stage will vary considerably according to the type of shrub: is it deciduous or evergreen? Is it a ground-cover plant? Is it grown

for its coloured winter stems or fruits? What is its natural growth habit? Some shrubs, such as *Potentilla*, will produce lots of thin, spindly stems while others, such as *Pyracantha*, will usually develop only a few strong, vigorous shoots. Small, very young plants will have produced less growth, so there is far less pruning to do than on an older, larger plant which may need quite a few branches and shoots removed to encourage the type of growth you want.

Deciduous shrubs are more likely to require formative pruning than evergreen ones, but with both types it is important to trim out any damaged shoots or roots (for those bought as bare-root specimens) as soon as possible. This is best done at the time of planting, which could be at any time of year for container-grown plants or during the dormant season for border-grown plants. After removing any damaged shoots and roots, lightly trim back any

dominant, over-vigorous shoots that spoil the shape and balance of the plant: remove about one third of the shoot (more severe pruning usually results in another strong shoot being produced to replace the old one). Finally, completely remove any spindly or crossing branches.

Training

Along with formative pruning, some training may be required, depending on the plant and how you intend to use it. Pruning and training are often closely linked because both are used in tandem to make a shrub grow in a particular way or to make a shoot grow in a certain direction.

Some shoots may be pruned lightly to encourage flower-bearing sideshoots to form, or more severely to promote new growth from the base of a shrub. Training, in terms of tying stems and shoots into a set position, is almost always required for shrubs grown against a wall or

Elaeagnus 'Quicksilver' and *Spiraea nipponica* 'Snowmound' both have fine shapes naturally, but pruning will constrain their vigorous growth.

In hot summers, magnolias may need dead-heading to prevent them forming seeds, but usually need little pruning.

fence, either because the shrub has a brittle root system (which is the case with many types of *Ceanothus*) or because the growth is very lax and straggling (as with *Callistemon*). (*See also* page 83.)

Where stem training is used, the most important point is the timing. Start the training when the shoots are semi-mature. At this stage, the growth is not so soft that the shoots are easily damaged when you bend them, and not so hard and woody that you cannot get them into position. Even in the case of some freestanding shrubs, training branches horizontally can substantially increase the amount of flower and fruit the plant will carry; also, by changing the apical dominance of a shoot (*see* page 13), you can encourage sideshoots to develop lower down.

Maintenance pruning

If you have taken care with the formative pruning stage, you should have a well-balanced, healthy plant with a good structure. Pruning from now on is about maintaining the balance of growth and encouraging the plant to do what you planted it for – for example, to produce plenty of flowers or fruit.

With many shrubs, this maintenance (routine) pruning will need to be done most years to varying degrees. The 'four Ds' (*see* page 19) are the place to start: remove any dead, damaged,

diseased or dying wood. Ideally this should be done every year, even if it is the only pruning that is done. Follow up by thinning out over-crowded or weak stems, and any stems that cross through the centre of the shrub. This is important not just for aesthetic reasons: crossing stems often rub against other shoots or stems, causing injury to both. It is a good idea to prune the strongest stems as well – to make sure that one very vigorous stem does not totally dominate the growth and create a shrub with an unbalanced shape.

One part of maintenance pruning that can confuse gardeners is sucker removal. A few shrubs will have been grafted onto a rootstock; these include some rhododendrons, roses, *Corylus avellana* 'Contorta' (corkscrew hazel) and *Hamamelis* (witch hazels). The rootstock onto

Don't forget

Dead-heading to remove spent flowers and prevent plants from forming seeds (*see* page 30) is all part of routine pruning, and for some shrubs it is all the regular pruning they need. Lilacs (*Syringa*) are usually dead-headed after flowering and often that is the only pruning they get for many years.

which they are grafted may produce sucker growths that need to be removed (*see* page 33). Other shrubs, such as *Clerodendrum trichotomum*, *Diervilla* and *Rubus cockburnianus* (whitewash bramble), have a naturally suckering habit, but they do not produce suckers in the true sense because they have not been grafted. The suckers are produced not by a different rootstock but by the plant itself, so in most cases these do not need to be removed. If you are not sure whether a sucker is truly a sucker (and therefore should be removed), try to establish whether or not the shrub has been grafted. The label is unlikely to tell you, but if you examine the base of the plant you can usually see the point at which the scion of the variety has been grafted onto the thicker, knobbly rootstock. There will be a fairly distinct 'graft union'.

Plants that have variegated foliage or flowers may need an additional type of pruning. Shoots with non-variegated foliage may emerge and quickly dominate the growth of the plant; these 'reverted' shoots should be removed as soon as they are spotted (*see* page 15).

Deciduous shrubs

Deciduous shrubs fall into four basic pruning groups:

Group 1: Shrubs that require little or no pruning.
Group 2: Shrubs that usually flower on the previous season's wood and are pruned in summer after flowering.
Group 3: Shrubs that flower on current season's growth and are pruned in spring.
Group 4: Shrubs that have a naturally suckering habit.

Group 1

Shrubs that need little or no regular pruning will generally grow and flower well for many years without much intervention from the gardener. *Chimonanthus*, *Cornus mas*, *C. florida* and many magnolias can be included in this group. With these shrubs pruning is required only to encourage the production of new shoots. Both *Rhus* and *Aralia* are often left unpruned, simply because they tend to produce large quantities of suckers that may spring up 2–3m (6–10ft) from the main stem; unfortunately, pruning often provokes these plants into producing even more suckers. Others, such as *Acer japonica* and *A. palmatum* (Japanese maples), usually need pruning only to remove any dead shoot tips (you might notice these after a frost, because they are susceptible to winter cold).

Group 1 deciduous shrubs

Acer japonicum, A. palmatum
Amelanchier
Aralia
Callistemon
Chimonanthus
Clethra
Colutea
Cornus florida, C. kousa, C. mas
Corylopsis
Cotinus (unless pruned for large leaves)
Cotoneaster (most, including *C. simonsii*, *C. franchetii* and *C. divaricatus*)
Daphne
Fothergilla
Hamamelis
Hibiscus syriacus
Magnolia
Prunus × cistena, P. incisa, P. pumila, P. tenella
Rhus
Stachyurus
Styrax
Syringa vulgaris cultivars
Viburnum

The diverse leaves of the shrubs in this border, from variegated *Cornus* to glossy evergreen *Choisya*, provide interest even when not in flower.

With both Japanese maples and magnolias, always try to wait until they are in full leaf before pruning; this will reduce 'bleeding' and the risk of infection from coral spot fungal disease (*see* pages 31–3).

Group 2

Shrubs that flower on the previous season's growth can be divided into two subgroups: those that flower in late winter or early spring, and those that flower in spring or summer.

Late winter or early spring

Shrubs that flower in late winter or early spring on wood produced in the previous season, such as *Prunus triloba*, are best pruned hard in spring, after flowering. Reduce the main stems by about half in the first spring after planting to form a basal framework. In subsequent years, cut

back all growth to two or three buds of the framework stems. Plants such as *Cotoneaster × watereri*, which are grown more for their brightly coloured berries in winter rather than their flowers, are also pruned in late winter or early spring, after the berries have been taken by the birds.

Sub-shrubs, and those shrubs that are fully frost hardy, such as *Artemisia* (wormwood), *Ceratostigma*, *Perovskia* and *Phygelius*, form a woody base. Such woody-based plants can be pruned back hard annually in spring, to stubs 15–30cm (6–12in) high, leaving one or two buds. Hardy fuchsias, such as *F. magellanica* and its cultivars, are also often pruned in this way. With many of these plants, it is prudent to wait until the growth has just started in order to assess the

Group 2 deciduous shrubs

Artemisia
Buddleja alternifolia
Ceanothus arboreus 'Trewithen Blue'
Ceratostigma
Chaenomeles
Cotoneaster × watereri (if grown for winter berries)
Deutzia
Forsythia
Hydrangea macrophylla
Kolkwitzia amabilis
Philadelphus
Prunus triloba
Ribes sanguineum
Spiraea 'Arguta', S. thunbergii
Stephanandra
Syringa meyeri 'Palibin', S. × persica
Tamarix tetrandra
Weigela

amount of winter damage and prune out any shoots that are not showing signs of new growth.

HOW TO prune shrubs that flower on the previous season's growth (Group 2)

1. After planting, or in the first spring, shorten the main stems by two thirds and any lateral shoots to two or three buds to form a good framework. In the second spring, cut out any thin, weak shoots and overcrowded stems.

2. In subsequent years, immediately after flowering, cut out about one in five of the stems (usually the oldest) close to ground level. Shorten flowering shoots on the stronger-growing stems to two to four buds.

Some shrubs (such as the flowering quince; here, *Chaenomeles speciosa*) flower better if the sideshoots are cut back in midsummer to form flower-bearing spurs. Less vigorous shrubs that can't take hard pruning are best simply dead-headed after flowering.

Spring or early summer

Many of the deciduous shrubs that flower in spring or early summer, such as *Forsythia*, carry their flowers on last year's wood. Other shrubs in this group, such as *Deutzia*, *Philadelphus* and *Weigela*, develop short sideshoots on last year's wood, and these in turn will carry the current season's flowers.

After planting, or in the first spring, remove any dead, damaged or diseased wood and shorten any thin, weak stems by two thirds. In the second spring, cut out any thin, weak shoots and thin out any overcrowded stems.

The natural tendency of many of the shrubs in this group is either to produce very strong, vigorous shoots (which can make the plant appear top-heavy because most of the foliage and all of the flowers will be carried on the top half of these stems), or to develop large amounts of dense, twiggy growth, especially towards the base. Maintenance pruning should be carried out immediately after flowering. The aim is to coax the plant into producing replacement shoots, by cutting out up to 20 per cent of the oldest stems each year to within 5–8cm (2–3in) of the ground.

With some shrubs that flower on the previous season's wood, their growth habit means they require little or no regular pruning, so they are often classified in Group 1. However, regular pruning can be carried out to encourage flowering. For example, *Chaenomeles* (flowering quince) has a naturally twiggy branch structure, with numerous branches and a straggling habit. It will do very well without pruning, but the flowering performance can be greatly improved if you cut sideshoots back to three to five leaves in midsummer: by doing this you create flower-bearing spurs.

With shrubs such as *Syringa* (lilacs) and hydrangeas, great care needs to be taken when pruning, because the new shoots – which will carry next year's flowers – form just below the existing flowers. These new shoots develop as the flowers are opening. When the time comes for dead-heading, the new shoots will often be around 15cm (6in) in length and all too easily fall casualty to a careless dead-heading session.

Group 3

This group of shrubs, which flower on the current season's growth, often produce lots of thin, spindly shoots and have a tendency to become overcrowded. This can lead to a gradual deterioration in the quantity and quality of the flowers, so some shoot thinning is usually necessary. The bigger shrubs in this group, such as the deciduous *Ceanothus*, will develop a framework of larger woody branches, so formative pruning is particularly important to create a good, balanced structure (*see* opposite).

Maintenance pruning should be carried out in spring, when new growth is emerging but not yet producing the vigorous shoots that will carry the flowers (in summer or early autumn). If you prune later you are likely to lose much of the flowering potential. The other advantage to pruning at this time is that, as the new growth emerges, it is very easy to spot and remove any soft, young autumn shoots that have been killed by winter frosts.

With maintenance pruning of Group 3 deciduous shrubs, the general rule is to reduce the main

Group 3 deciduous shrubs

Buddleja davidii cultivars
Caryopteris × *clandonensis* cultivars
Ceanothus 'Gloire de Versailles',
C. 'Perle Rose'
Clerodendrum bungei
Fuchsia
Hydrangea paniculata
Lavatera
Perovskia
Spartium junceum
Tamarix ramosissima

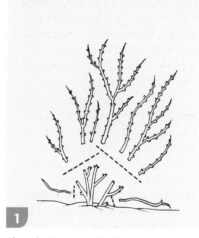

1 After planting, or in the first spring, encourage a good framework of branches by shortening all of the main stems by two thirds and cutting back any laterals to two or three buds.

2 In the second spring, reduce the previous year's growth by about half its length. Remove any thin, weak, spindly shoots, and cut out one in three of any overcrowded shoots.

3 In subsequent years, completely remove any old or unproductive branches or stems to prevent overcrowding. Reduce the main stems by one third and cut back the lateral shoots to two or three buds.

stems by one third and cut back the lateral shoots to two or three buds: always remove completely any old or unproductive shoots to prevent overcrowding and to allow space for new growths to develop.

Group 4

Shrubs with a suckering habit produce young shoots as suckers from around the base of the original plant at soil level, and have a

Group 4 deciduous shrubs

Clerodendrum trichotomum
Cytisus scoparius and hybrids
Diervilla
Kerria japonica, K. j. 'Golden Guinea'
Leycesteria formosa
Rubus cockburnianus
Sambucus

tendency to spread. These suckers are part of their normal growth and not a problem as they are on roses (*see* page 86).

These shrubs produce their flowers on the previous year's wood, and should be pruned as soon as the flowers have faded, by cutting out as much of the old flower-bearing growth as possible. The new young shoots are usually a vivid green and brighten the garden in winter.

Coppicing

Sometimes called stooling, coppicing involves cutting a plant down to just above ground level in spring in order to make it produce vigorous new shoots. (For coppicing trees, *see* page 40.)

The technique is used on plants that are grown not for their flowers

but for their colourful juvenile stems. In some cases, coppicing also results in the growth of leaves that are three or four times the normal size, creating an even bolder display. Coppicing may also be used to rejuvenate old, tired shrubs (such as *Buddleja*), as long as they will tolerate hard pruning. (For shrubs that can be coppiced for shoots and/ or leaves, *see* box on page 54.)

When you first plant a shrub that you intend to coppice, trim it lightly (remove the end third of each shoot), and remove any dead, dying, damaged or diseased growth. Don't try to coppice a shrub in its first year. This is important, because this formative light prune will allow the plant to develop a strong root system before maintenance pruning begins.

HOW TO coppice a shrub

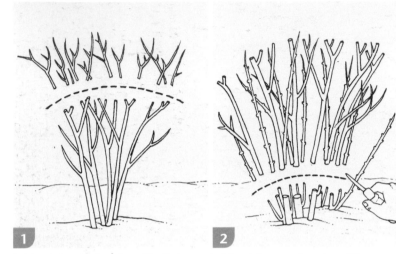

1 In late winter or early spring of the first growing season, cut the stem or stems back to just above a bud or a pair of buds, reducing the overall height by about one third. Cut all thin, weak shoots back to the stem or to the ground.

2 In late winter or early spring of the second growing season, prune all stems back to 5–8cm (2–3in) above ground level. After this, coppice the most vigorous plants annually, others every two or three years, as needed.

Don't forget

Coppicing can be very exhausting for a plant, so each time you do it give the plant a generous helping of fertilizer followed by a mulch of garden compost or manure (*see* page 31).

Routine coppicing is carried out in late winter or early spring. Cut the strongest, thickest stems back to just above a bud or a pair of buds 5–10cm (2–4in) above ground level. Remove completely any thin, weak stems by cutting them back to the stem or to the ground. This routine coppicing can be carried out annually with plants that will tolerate very hard pruning. For others you need to adjust the regime. For example, some types of dogwood (such as *Cornus stolonifera*) should be pruned hard only in alternate years, as they do not have the vigour to cope with hard pruning on an annual basis in the same way that *C. alba* and its cultivars can. With plants like this you can phase the pruning: cut two thirds of the stems back to a low level each year, leaving one third unpruned (these are pruned hard the following year). This way, there are always some mature stems carrying plenty of leaves to manufacture food for the whole plant. This appears to keep the plants healthier and more vigorous for longer than plants that are pruned severely every year.

After several years of coppicing a plant, some old, knotty stumps may start to develop; remove these using a saw or loppers to start new growths from the base of the plant.

Coppicing for renovation

While coppicing is usually done to achieve a special effect, it is sometimes necessary in order to rejuvenate a shrub that has been neglected. However, it will only work with shrubs that tolerate hard pruning, such as *Buddleja*.

In late winter or early spring, cut all growth down to ground level. As new shoots emerge in late spring, leave only the thickest and strongest; remove all thin, weak stems, and thin out overcrowded shoots by cutting out two thirds of them as low down as possible.

In the following year, leave several large stems and prune the remainder back to 5–8cm (2–3in) above ground level. In the second year after renovation pruning, you

Most hebes (here, *H.* 'Watson's Pink') can tolerate hard pruning. They will grow more vigorously and look neater if faded flower spikes are removed and lanky stems are cut back.

can resume the programme of maintenance pruning.

Evergreen shrubs

As a general rule, evergreen shrubs tend to need far less formative pruning than their deciduous counterparts. The aim is to produce a plant with even, balanced growth with the minimum amount of pruning. Ideally this pruning should be carried out in mid-spring or soon after the shrub has been planted. However, if you've planted in autumn, defer the pruning until spring to avoid the chance of new growths being damaged by frost. It is worth remembering that evergreens have two main periods of growth – one in mid-spring and another in late summer – and although the mature growth on most evergreen plants is perfectly hardy, soft, tender young growths are very easily damaged by frost or wind chill.

For established evergreen shrubs, relatively minimal maintenance pruning is required, although there are specific requirements to take into account depending on the type of shrub (*see* pages 56–8). Generally, as with most other plants, start with any visible dead, damaged, dying and diseased wood, cutting back to a point where there are either signs of new growth starting to emerge or to a

point where live, healthy tissue can be seen (*see* page 19). Once this essential pruning has been done, you can move on to remedial work such as thinning out overcrowded or rubbing shoots, and removing or shortening any large, vigorous shoots that distort the balance and shape of the plant, and to restrict overall size if space is limited. The aim is to develop an open-centred plant with evenly spaced branches (although this tends to happen anyway as the leaves and small branches in the centre of the plant usually die owing to lack of light). Some shrubs tolerate hard pruning (*see* box, right); others don't.

Evergreen shrubs that tolerate hard pruning

Berberis darwinii

Buxus

Escallonia rubra and cultivars

Eucalyptus

Griselinia littoralis

Hebe

Ilex

Ligustrum

Lonicera nitida

Mahonia

Olearia

Prunus laurocerasus, P. lusitanica and cultivars

Pyracantha

Rhododendron

Taxus

Prunus laurocerasus 'Otto Luyken' is ideal for an informal hedge, producing glossy evergreen leaves that are studded with cockades of white flowers in spring and a few more in autumn.

Many evergreen shrubs are grown for their variegated foliage, and on these plants any shoots that have green-only leaves (no variegation) must be removed so that the plant does not revert to its green-leaved form (*see* page 15). This may pose a problem, as broad-leaved evergreens are often planted under trees and, when light levels are lower, plants with variegated foliage naturally tend to revert to their green-leaved form. Also remove any shoots that have no green in them at all, as is often the case with variegated holly (*Ilex*) cultivars. These all-cream or all-white shoots have no chlorophyll, so are unable to manufacture food, and are being kept alive by the variegated leaves on the rest of the plant.

For pruning purposes, evergreen shrubs can be divided into three groups: large, medium and small.

Large evergreen shrubs: over 3m (10ft) in height

This group includes *Camellia japonica* cultivars, *Garrya elliptica* (silk-tassel bush), *Ilex* cultivars (holly), *Photinia*, *Prunus laurocerasus* (laurel) and other tall evergreens that need very little regular pruning, but may require some formative pruning when young to create a balanced framework. Formative pruning may be needed for up to three years, depending on the habit and growth rate of the plant. Ideally, maintenance pruning would be carried out annually, but often alternate years will be sufficient.

Some plants within the large and medium groups are grown more for their seasonal foliage than for their flowers. The spring foliage on the new shoots is brightly coloured,

with shades of orange and red for *Photinia* and pink, cream or red for *Pieris*, depending on the cultivar. As they mature, these new shoots gradually turn green. Both of these shrubs can be pruned in spring after flowering (in both cases the flowers come after the brightly coloured new shoots). Removing these new growths and the old flowerheads helps to produce a better display of both foliage and flowers in the following year.

Formative In mid-spring, cut out any weak and crossing branches; the aim is to create a plant with an evenly spaced framework of branches and an open centre. For those shrubs that flower from midsummer onwards, dead-head after the flowers have finished.

Maintenance Cut out any dead, damaged and diseased wood in spring and remove thin, straggly shoots; cut back by about one third any strong, vigorous shoots that give the plant an unbalanced appearance. For those shrubs that flower from midsummer onwards, dead-head after the flowers have finished, taking care not to damage any of the new shoots. With camellias and rhododendrons, the new shoots often develop just below the flower buds as the flowers open and this can make pruning difficult.

Medium evergreen shrubs: 1–3m (3–10ft) in height

This group includes *Aucuba japonica* cultivars (spotted laurel), *Berberis × stenophylla* (evergreen barberry), *Escallonia* and *Osmanthus*.

The shrubs in this group that flower during winter or spring, such as *Berberis darwinii*, *Mahonia japonica*, *Skimmia* and *Viburnum tinus*, need pruning immediately after flowering – as a rough guide, take out any shoots that have dead flowers on them. Where the fruits are being kept for added interest, prune in the following year, just before the new flush of flowers opens on the next generation of branches.

The shrubs in this group that flower from midsummer onwards are pruned in mid-spring, after the risk of severe frost has passed: cut out old stems, and then in late summer remove flowered stems. If a plant flowers into autumn, prune it the following spring. This treatment is suitable for shrubs such as *Escallonia*, *Olearia macrodonta* (daisy bush) and *Osmanthus heterophyllus* (false holly).

Formative In spring, as the new growth starts, remove completely any weak, spindly shoots and cut back by one third any very strong, vigorous stems. This will encourage new shoots to grow from low down and check any strong shoots that may dominate the growth and shape of the shrub. (This process can also be repeated in the second year after planting.) During summer, remove any weak, crossing shoots; cutting out the flower buds in the first year after planting encourages the plant to establish more quickly.

Maintenance For evergreen shrubs that flower in winter or spring, prune immediately after flowering. Remove the dead flowers (unless berries are desired), and cut out thin, straggly shoots. In summer, trim back any very vigorous shoots by one third.

For shrubs that produce flowers from midsummer, remove the dead flowers along with a section of stem in late summer or early autumn. (In exposed areas, this may be delayed until early spring.)

Small evergreen shrubs: up to 1m (3ft) in height

These shrubs can be divided into two distinct groups: owing to their growth habit, each requires different methods of pruning.

Group 1 This group comprises a number of shrubs that are not fully hardy and are relatively short-lived (generally about ten years or so), as well as a number that have a coating of hairs over the foliage, making them very vulnerable to cold, wet winters. These include *Calluna* (heather), *Daboecia* (heath), *Erica* (heather, low-growing forms), *Lavandula* (lavender), *Santolina chamaecyparissus* (cotton lavender), *Phygelius* (Cape figwort) and *Salvia officinalis* (sage).

The best time to prune is mid- to late spring, and maybe even later in cold areas, where there is a risk of

severe or late frosts. Much of the pruning involves removing any frost-damaged growths before taking out any thin, weak growth and all old flowering shoots. Although they flower profusely, if not trimmed annually these plants tend to become bare or cluttered with dead stems in the centre of the plant, often leaving an open, sprawling mess.

Formative pruning for this group begins in spring (or soon after planting). Reduce all stems by two thirds of their original length. This will encourage lots of new shoots, to give fresh new growth to work with. In summer, if these shoots are overcrowded, trim out the thinnest, weakest shoots to favour

Pieris 'Firecrest' needs little pruning other than the removal of dead or badly placed shoots immediately after flowering.

the strongest stems and give a well-balanced framework.

In subsequent years, as the new growth begins in spring, prune out all dead, damaged or diseased shoots; cut out all the old flowering shoots, and remove all thin, weak growths to generate new growth from the base at the centre of the plant.

After flowering, cut out any dead or damaged shoots and remove the old flower-bearing stems. With lavender, which tends to become leggy and bare at the base, if you dead-head after flowering but remove the top two pairs of leaves along with the dead flower and flower stalk, this will encourage thick, bushy growth; then the only pruning needed in spring is to remove any frost-damaged growth (there should be far less of this, owing to the tightly branched growth achieved by pruning after flowering).

Group 2 This group includes shrubs with a slow to moderately vigorous growth rate, often with a suckering habit, such as *Cotoneaster horizontalis*, *Genista lydia* (Spanish gorse), *Hypericum calycinum* (rose of Sharon), *Mahonia aquifolium* (Oregon grape) and *Ruscus aculeatus* (butcher's broom). They are far less of a challenge than Group 1 shrubs: they require little or no regular pruning, and even dead-heading is not necessary if the plants are grown for their attractive berries in autumn and winter. However, as with most woody plants, they do require some formative pruning: after planting, cut back all shoots by two thirds.

The main purpose of maintenance pruning the plants in this group is to remove any dead flowers, to keep the plants dense and bushy (by giving them a light trim, usually after flowering), or to remove dead,

damaged or diseased shoots. Such shoots must be cut to ground level in mid-spring; also cut back any thin, weak growths (this will promote new growth from the centre of the plant and, in plants that have a suckering habit, encourage it to multiply).

Renovating shrubs

Most old, neglected, or straggly shrubs respond to severe pruning, so they can be renovated. If there are any doubts, the best approach is to use 'phased renovation' pruning (*see* opposite). Rather than cutting down the entire plant, cut back half or one third in order to let the pruned section start some regrowth before pruning another section. This process may take two or three years, but it is better than killing the plant. *Senecio* (syn. *Brachyglottis*) and *Callistemon* (bottlebrush) both respond well to this treatment. With deciduous and evergreen shrubs covering such a large group of plants from many different plant families, however, it is hard to generalize about what is the best course of action when it comes to trying to salvage an unkempt plant by renovation pruning.

How will a shrub respond?

Some shrubs respond to hard pruning by producing new, vigorous young growth from the base, or even from below soil level. This is not always good, though; with *Syringa* (lilac) cultivars it is actually

Train or shorten the spreading, stiff stems of *Cotoneaster horizontalis* regularly, because it does not renovate well if it becomes overgrown.

1

In late winter or early spring, cut up to half of the main stems to the base or to a low framework, concentrating on badly placed, old, and diseased wood. Shorten the rest by up to half their length. The aim is encourage growth from the base.

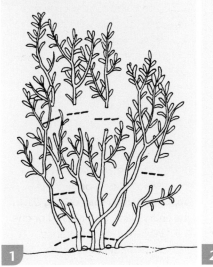

2

The following year, cut back half of the remaining main stems to ground level or the low framework. Thin the new shoots that formed as a result of pruning in Step 1. Leave the strongest shoots on the remains of the thickest stubs to form a new shrub.

3

in the third year, cut any remaining old stems that have produced either no new stems or only thin, weak growths down to soil level.

4

Further growths may appear from the old stumps from time to time for several years. Prune these out, or pull them away if you spot them while they are still soft.

a bad sign on old plants because many are propagated by grafting, which means that such hard pruning can result in suckers growing from the rootstock (in this case *Syringa vulgaris*), rather than from the cultivar grafted on top (*see also* page 33). Even worse, some plants will die rather than regenerate after renovation pruning.

Some shrubs just fail to produce new growth from old wood if they are pruned severely. Deciduous *Ceanothus* respond well, but evergreen *Ceanothus* rarely regrow. *Cytisus* (broom) and *Lavandula* (lavender) simply do not respond; even though the wood may be alive several years after pruning, it does not produce new shoots. *Spartium junceum* is totally unpredictable – sometimes it regrows, other times it does not. Many shrubs display remarkable powers of recovery, however, and with drastic pruning can be rejuvenated in a relatively short period of time (*see* page 55). After two or three years, as the shrub recovers from this drastic pruning and starts to resume its normal growth pattern, prune it as often as appropriate, depending on its growth habit and flowering season.

Is it worth the effort?

If a shrub is badly damaged or diseased, it may be necessary to dig it up and start again with a new specimen. It is also worth considering whether or not you have the right plant in the right place – if the plant was a poor selection for its situation in the first place it should really be removed and replaced with something more appropriate.

| # Training a standard

Plants trained as standards often command high prices in nurseries and garden centres, which can make them appear too difficult or specialized for the home gardener to attempt. But the price usually reflects the time it takes for the classic evergreen standards of box or bay (*Buxus* or *Laurus nobilis*) to reach their full glory, which is often several years. You can try these if that's what you yearn for, but if you prefer more rapid results, you could start with faster-growing flowering shrubs. Fuchsias will show you success in a year or two, making them a perfect practice plant – and attractive in their own right.

To keep a fuchsia flowering for years, simply cut back the previous year's growth when new shoots emerge in the crown in spring.

Start with a well-rooted cutting with a good, straight central stem, and strip off any sideshoots to leave only the main stem or leader.

Transfer the cutting into a 10cm (4in) pot to grow on, and push in a short houseplant cane alongside it to provide support for the stem as it extends. Tie in the lengthening stem to the cane every 10cm (4in) so that it grows as straight as possible, and remove shoots that appear along the lower part of the stem before they become too large.

When the pot is filled with roots and the stem has reached the top of the cane, repot into a 15cm (6in) pot. Replace the houseplant cane with a 1m (40in) bamboo cane, and leave the plant to grow on as before. When the stem has reached the top of the cane, pinch out the growing tip. This stops upward growth and encourages sideshoots (*see* page 13). Remove any sideshoots on the clear stem, but let those that form just below the tip grow to about 5cm (2in), and then pinch them out in turn. From now on, just

keep pinching out the tips of those shoots when the new sideshoots reach about 5cm (2in), building up a large, dense, spherical head. When it is large enough, stop pinching, and your standard will flower at the usual time.

1 Remove all sideshoots from the rooted cutting. Transfer the cutting to a new, slightly larger pot to grow on.

2 Tie the stem to a cane to make sure the plant is well supported as it grows and develops an upright habit.

3 Keep pinching out sideshoots until the required height is reached and regularly tie in the extending stem.

Hedges

Many trees and shrubs can be used to create a hedge – after all, a hedge is really just a row of woody plants growing closely together, each one growing into its neighbours to create a continuous barrier. A good hedge plant is one that will respond positively to regular close clipping by producing lots of small branches that grow together to form a dense, interlocking screen of shoots.

Hedging styles

There is a vast range of ornamental plants that can be used for hedges, both evergreen and deciduous. The overall effect can be formal or informal, and uniform or tapestry-like, using a diverse mixture of different types of plant.

Formal hedges

Hedges that are frequently clipped or pruned to form a living screen or barrier of densely branching foliage are referred to as formal hedges. They may need to be clipped several times a year to give the desired effect. These hedges are often formed from plants that are more noted for their foliage or 'prickliness' rather than for their flowering performance, and include *Taxus* (yew), *Ilex* (holly), *Prunus laurocerasus* (laurel), *Fagus* (beech) and *Crataegus* (hawthorn).

Pleaching, in which the top branches of trees are woven together above clear trunks, is the most labour-intensive form of hedge pruning. A pleached hedge can take up to 15 years to become established and requires regular trimming.

Informal hedges

Hedges that are more like a row of shrubs placed close together are known as informal hedges, and often include flowering subjects that are allowed to produce long flower-bearing shoots before they are pruned. These hedges tend to be pruned rather than clipped in the way that formal hedges normally are. With some species, such as *Chaenomeles* (flowering quince) and *Rosa rugosa* (Ramanas rose), which produce attractive fruits, some pruning is carried out in late winter or early spring to remove the old, fruit-bearing shoots.

Mixed or tapestry hedges

Most commonly, a hedge is made up of one type of plant to give it a degree of uniformity and formality, but you can also get hedges created from several different species of plant. These can be arranged randomly along the hedge line; this is quite common for hedges where native plants are used and often a mixture to reflect the local vegetation is chosen. Alternatively, a set arrangement may be used; this can be a predetermined sequence, such as one golden-leaved plant after every three green-leaved ones.

These 'mixed' or 'tapestry' hedges are often created from plants that have been selected to provide a variety of colours and effects throughout the year. For example, you could mix different leaf colours, shapes and textures, both flowering and non-flowering species, or different growth habits including evergreen and deciduous subjects. Other plants may

An unusual effect is created here with willow (*Salix*), pruned and trained to become what could be described as a cross between a fence and a hedge.

be included because they produce colourful fruits – for instance, *Pyracantha* (firethorn) gives a choice of berry colour with shades of yellow, orange and red. An added advantage to many fruiting plants is that they attract birds to the garden.

While mixed or tapestry hedges can provide some very colourful combinations and effects, they are more difficult to manage than a more traditional hedge. This is simply because no two species of plant ever grow at the same rate, so clipping and trimming can be more difficult than with a hedge made from a single plant species. The different growth rates also mean that this type of hedge will never look as tidy as a single species hedge, so these hedges are usually informal and are not clipped as hard or as frequently as formal hedges.

Cloud hedges
A cloud hedge is a large, established hedge that has been clipped regularly, but – rather than being shaped into the standard formal hedge with straight sides and a flat top – has been treated like a row of topiary plants. With this technique, which originated in Japan, the hedge is allowed to flow into curves and waves, but is still tightly clipped. To gain the full effect you need to use plants such as *Buxus* (box) and *Taxus* (yew), which will cope with the close clipping.

Formative pruning
Many gardeners are loath to prune a young hedge, preferring to wait until the plants have established. Quite often this means that the initial formative pruning never actually gets done. You can see this where there are gaps through a hedge at soil level and the stems of the original plants can clearly be seen, even in coniferous hedges. Such hedges do not provide an effective barrier.

Plants for hedges

FORMAL HEDGES
Berberis thunbergii (deciduous)
Buxus sempervirens (evergreen)
Carpinus betulus (deciduous)
Chamaecyparis lawsoniana (evergreen)
Crataegus monogyna (deciduous)
Elaeagnus × ebbingei (evergreen)
Escallonia (evergreen)
Fagus sylvatica (deciduous)
Griselinia littoralis (evergreen)
Ilex aquifolium (evergreen)
Lavandula (evergreen)
Ligustrum (evergreen)
Lonicera nitida (evergreen)
Prunus laurocerasus (evergreen)
Pyracantha (evergreen)
Taxus baccata (evergreen)
Thuja plicata (evergreen)

INFORMAL HEDGES
Berberis darwinii (evergreen)
Berberis thunbergii (deciduous)
Cotoneaster lacteus (evergreen)
Crataegus monogyna (deciduous)
Escallonia (evergreen)
Forsythia × intermedia (deciduous)
Fuchsia magellanica (deciduous)
Garrya elliptica (evergreen)
Ilex aquifolium (evergreen)
Lavandula (evergreen)
Pyracantha (evergreen)
Rosa rugosa (deciduous)
Viburnum tinus (evergreen)

A cloud hedge of holly (*Ilex*). Several people who have this type of hedge readily admit that their 'cloud hedge' started life as a formal hedge that grew out of shape, and they preferred the informal lines as they developed.

For a good hedge to form, the growth in the early stages of development should be slow and steady. This will provide short spaces between the shoots, creating a mass of dense, compact branches. So avoid trying to get the shoot tips up to the desired height in the shortest possible time. Unless you have planted large, mature specimens to form your hedge (and you can buy instant hedges these days), the first three years tend to be critical in forming the shape you desire and developing a good spreading root system to support the hedge in future years.

As a general rule, soon after planting remove the top third of the plants' overall height to encourage dense, bushy growth from ground level upwards; with deciduous plants it pays to wait until the young plants have started to grow before cutting them back, then you can spot any dead shoots and remove those at the same time. Also prune the sides or 'faces' of the hedge to trim back long, straggling growths by half their length; this will encourage the shoots growing along the hedge line to grow into one another and 'knit' together to form a hedge unit rather than just a row of individual plants.

Usually, formative pruning (see right and page 64) varies little for the first three years after the hedge has been planted.

(see right and page 64)

Don't forget

If you want a tall hedge, there may come a stage when you are carrying out formative pruning on the top third of the young hedge and simultaneously undertaking maintenance pruning on the established lower levels of the same hedge.

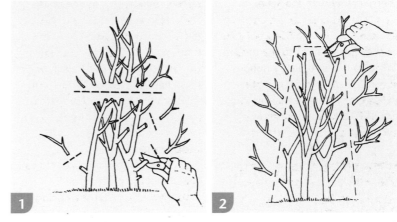

HOW TO prune an evergreen hedge (formative)

For clarity, the leaves are not shown in these illustrations.

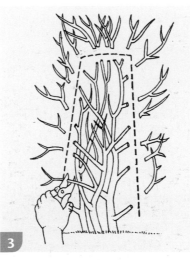

1 Plant evergreen hedging plants about 30–60cm (12–24in) apart, ideally in spring or early autumn. In their first spring, cut back the plants by about one third of their original height and trim back any long, straggling shoots growing out at right angles to the hedge line (the faces of the hedge).

2 In the first summer or autumn, lightly prune any shoots that are growing out at right angles to the line of the hedge. This will encourage more branching from sideshoots and encourage the plants to grow into one another. Prune back hard any strong, vigorous shoots that spoil the shape and line of the hedge.

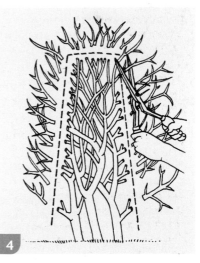

3 In the second year, in spring or summer, reduce upright shoots by about one third of their length to encourage horizontal growth. As the new shoots develop, trim back any shoots growing out at right angles to the hedge to keep the habit dense and bushy.

4 In the third year, in summer or autumn, start trimming the hedge to shape. Continue to prune back any shoots that spoil the line and remove the top third of upright shoots. Later, when the hedge has reached its intended height, prune the top down to 30cm (12in) below this height.

HOW TO prune a deciduous hedge (formative)

1

In the first winter or early spring, just before growth starts, cut the plants back to about half their original height and trim back any long, straggling shoots growing at right angles to the hedge line (the faces of the hedge). Also, remove any dead shoots and trim back damaged stems. In the first summer or autumn, prune as for an evergreen hedge (*see* step 2, page 63).

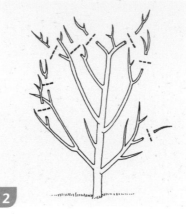

2

In the second winter, cut back by about one third all of the new growths; also, shorten any side branches and shoots that spoil the shape and line of the hedge. In summer, as the new shoots develop, trim back any shoots growing at right angles to the hedge. In the third year, in summer or autumn, prune as for an evergreen hedge (*see* step 4, page 63).

Maintaining a hedge

Pruning a hedge regularly is usually referred to as 'clipping' or 'trimming', especially when dealing with formal hedges, because it is a slightly different type of pruning that involves cutting back soft, sappy shoots several times during the growing season. This type of pruning is used to produce a network of small, multi-branched shoots over the entire surface of the hedge; initially this will just be the sides and possibly the ends of the hedge, but when the hedge has grown to the desired height the top surface will be treated in the same way.

Size and shape

The size of any hedge, in terms of width and height, is usually limited by accessibility – basically, how far you can reach upwards to trim the sides and ends of a hedge and how far you can reach across the top to cut it. There is no point in having a hedge so wide that you are not able to reach the middle from either side of the hedge. Even a tall hedge can be quite narrow, not needing to be any wider than 75cm (2½ft) at the base, but this will depend on good formative pruning to maintain a narrow profile to start with. Plant selection can also have a bearing, not so much on the ultimate size of the hedge, but on how frequently it has to be trimmed to limit its growth to the proportions you had in mind when you planned it.

The sides

As a general rule, it is better to have a hedge with tapered sides (*see* below). From a practical point of view, it makes trimming easier and it usually makes the entire surface area of the hedge accessible to daylight, which promotes even growth and produces a better overall effect. The sloping angle of the hedge is called the 'batter'. If a hedge is wider at the top than at the base, the overhang will shade some parts of the sides; the growth in these areas will become weak and sparsely covered, and sections may even die owing to lack of light.

The top

If you can, avoid a flat top to your hedge since it can create far too many problems. Prunings can accumulate on the flat surface (rather than fall

Ideally, a hedge will be narrower at the top than at the base. Sloping sides will deflect winds, snow will fall away down the sides and the base will be exposed to sunlight.

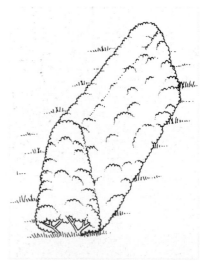

away from a top with sloping sides).
If these prunings are not completely
removed they may start to ferment
and rot, which causes the death of
living shoots in the top of the hedge;
it may also encourage pests and
diseases to colonize the dead and
dying areas, which can be a serious
problem with hedges made from
coniferous and evergreen plants. In
winter, snow may mount up on the
flat surface and the weight may cause
the branches to spread out or splay;
this can damage the branches and
ruin the profile of the hedge.

Clipping the hedge

You can save time and do a better
job of clipping a formal hedge if you
plan beforehand how you intend to
tackle it. Where possible, spread out
a ground sheet of some kind, with
one edge tucked just under the edge
of the hedge. This will catch the

Here, formal hedge-clipping
techniques have been used to prune
yew (*Taxus baccata*) to create an
alcove rather than a boundary.

clippings, making it much easier to
collect up afterwards.

Start cutting from the base of the
hedge in an upwards direction, so
that the prunings fall clear of the
section you are working on – this
makes it much easier to see what you
are cutting. If you notice any thick
shoots that may be too thick for
shears or a hedge trimmer, cut these
back with secateurs first, and cut
back slightly further than the
intended surface of the hedge so
that the thick branch stubs do not
later come into contact with the
cutters and jam them.

Use secateurs for clipping hedges
made from broad-leaved evergreens
such as *Ilex* (holly), *Prunus*

This lovely copper beech hedge (*Fagus
sylvatica* Atropurpurea group, shown
here in spring) produces rich-purple
leaves that turn coppery in autumn.

laurocerasus (laurel) and *P. lusitanica*
(Portuguese laurel), because these
have large leaves that are often
mutilated by shears and hedge
trimmers, with the damaged leaves
subsequently turning yellow and
falling off. For large hedges made
from these plants, hand clipping may
not be practical, in which case trim
with shears early in the season so
that the new spring growth quickly
hides the yellowing leaves. (For
information on hedge-clipping tools,
see pages 22–7).

Unless you are trying to create a
'cloud hedge' (*see* page 62), there
are few things that attract the eye
better than an uneven top to a
hedge; even a well-maintained
hedge looks less attractive if the top
is not level, or (on a sloping site)

Once you've 'got your eye in' you will be able to clip hedges quite symmetrically without the aid of a taut line. But always clip the sides first and then the top.

follows the contours of the land. The easiest way to get an even top to a hedge is to stretch a highly visible, brightly coloured string or garden line between two posts, with the correct height measured on the posts; do this after the sides have been cut so that you can get the line close to the hedge before you start cutting the top.

As you clip the growth on the top of the hedge, cut from the outside, inwards towards the centre, regularly brushing the clippings from the hedge top onto the ground sheet.

Renovating a hedge

Hedges are living communities of plants fiercely competing with one another for water, nutrients and light, with the added pressure of having large quantities of their foliage removed on a regular

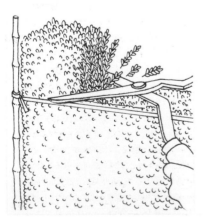

After the sides have been trimmed, set up a string at the desired height before starting to trim the top. As with the sides, cut back any thick branches and shoots before using the hedge trimmer. (If the top of the hedge is over chest height for the person trimming it, work from a platform so that the cutting is done at a comfortable height.)

basis – often several times a year. Even when a hedge is well cared for, well watered and regularly fed, the plants within the hedge may become diseased or damaged, suffer from stress, or just gradually become too large. One of the ways to remedy these problems is to renovate the hedge by severe pruning.

The way you renovate a hedge is usually determined by the plants growing within it. There are three main pruning groups for hedges,

depending on the type of plants you are growing:

Group 1: Plants that respond well to being cut down completely.

Group 2: Plants that can be pruned in stages to replace the old growth with new.

Group 3: Plants that do not have the capacity to generate new growth from old wood (including most conifers).

Group 1

Some plants can be cut down to just above ground level and they will regrow to form a new hedge. These include *Pyracantha* (firethorn), *Prunus laurocerasus* (laurel) and *Crataegus* (hawthorn). If you are recreating a hedge, once the plants start to grow you will need to follow the procedure for formative pruning (*see* pages 63–4).

Group 2

Plants such as *Fagus* (beech), *Carpinus* (hornbeam) and *Taxus* (yew) respond to a less severe pruning treatment. In the first year, cut back to the main stems all of the branches on one side of the hedge. In the following year, prune the other side of the hedge in the same way. In the third year, prune back the top of the hedge (including any new shoots) to about two thirds of the intended final height. The top of the hedge should always be pruned last to encourage new shoots to grow on the sides and lower sections of the hedge, rather than creating excessive growth on the top.

With broad-leaved evergreens, this pruning should be carried out in late spring. Deciduous species should be treated in late winter or early spring. For both types of plant, the timing is important, as they will put on a massive surge of growth at

A yew hedge (*Taxus*) has been drastically pruned to renovate it. Both sides have been cut hard back, but the hedge is young enough to respond favourably.

these times of year, which means that the plants concerned will respond very quickly.

For renovation to work, the plants reforming the hedge need to be treated as new young plants, and it is important to keep the hedge fed and well watered to promote rapid growth. Mulching the plants soon after pruning is also of great benefit, because the plants' roots may suffer from excessive heat after the hedge has been cut back and the shade provided by the branches has been removed. For the first year, it is important to examine the cut surfaces regularly to make sure that no fungal

infection has entered the pruning cuts. Any infected material should be removed and burned immediately.

Group 3

The plants that do not respond to renovation pruning, such as most conifers (except *Taxus baccata*), leave you no alternative but to remove an ailing or neglected hedge and plant another one. Until recently, replanting with the same species was always avoided because the new plants often suffered from 'replant disease' or 'soil sickness'. This can now be avoided by incorporating a preparation of beneficial bacteria and fungi into the soil just prior to planting.

To encourage the bright red young leaves of *Photinia* (here, *P. × fraseri* 'Red Robin'), shorten stems by up to 15cm (6in) when the plant is established. Photinias also respond well to renovation pruning (Group 1).

Topiary

Topiary is the ancient art of creating sculptures from living plants, usually evergreen trees and shrubs. You need patience, and an eye for design and shape, but once you have learnt the techniques the only limit to your creations is your imagination.

Traditional topiary has always been about creating strong, formal, geometric shapes – obelisks, columns, pyramids and cubes – by the frequent clipping and shaping of plants. More recently, shapes have come to include just about anything: animals, birds – even aeroplanes, trains and giant chess pieces. Of course, there will always be the topiary 'purist' who feels that these modern shapes are cheating, as they are often created with the aid of metal frames or structures, with the plant growths trained through them rather than pruned to shape.

Whichever method is used to create the shape, the fact remains that even a small topiary specimen requires a great deal of time, skill and patience to achieve, as well as dedication to maintain it once established. Topiary subjects can be created as freestanding specimens either in the garden or for growing in containers; or they can be sculpted from part of another garden feature, such as a formal hedge.

Whatever shape you are creating, it is vital to trim the plants at the right time of year. Pruning after late summer is not advisable, as soft young shoots are particularly vulnerable to frost damage in late autumn and winter. Topiary grown in pots may also be prone to root damage caused by frost, even though the stems and branches may be quite hardy, so insulating the rootball is always a wise precaution in cold areas.

Plant suitability

Plants for pruning into topiary need to be sufficiently dense in order to cover the whole surface area and give 'body' to the sculpture; they must also provide crisp, clean lines so that the shape is clearly defined.

Ideally, topiary plants should have small, evergreen leaves and a slow to medium growth habit, so that pruning and training are a frequent rather than constant task. Flexible stems make training easier, and plants that respond well to being regularly pruned tend to give the most satisfying results (*see* box, left). Plants should have a long life span and be tough and hardy. This will avoid the need to prune plants merely to remove and repair sections

Line, texture and contrast in form are the strong points of topiary.

that have been damaged by low temperatures and cold winds. It is worth remembering that the more vigorous plants will provide a fairly rapid result in terms of achieving a desired shape, but the drawback is that they will need more maintenance pruning than slower-growing cultivars. Shrubby honeysuckle (*Lonicera*) and privet (*Ligustrum*) will need to be clipped two or three (possibly more) times each year, whereas yew (*Taxus*) will require clipping only once or, at most, twice a year once the formative pruning has been completed.

Pruning methods

Topiary requires more precision than most other types of pruning. Clean, sharp tools are essential to get the best results, since most of the growth will be young and quite soft when it is pruned (a pruning regime of 'little and often' will achieve the best results in most cases). You'll need

Plants suitable for topiary

Artemisia abrotanum
Berberis darwinii
Buxus sempervirens
Cupressus sempervirens
Ilex aquifolium
Laurus nobilis
Ligustrum ovalifolium
Lonicera nitida
Olearia nummularifolia
Osmanthus heterophyllus
Phillyrea latifolia
Rosmarinus officinalis
Santolina chamaecyparissus
Taxus baccata

long-handled shears, secateurs, and some topiary shears. Having said this, one of the most useful tools is your finger and thumb – some of the best topiary pruning is done by pinching out the growing points with fingernails.

Creating the shapes

Rounded or curved shapes are much easier to create and maintain than shapes with sharp, clearly defined edges (such as a pyramid). So if you have never tried topiary before, start with rounded shapes.

One of the classic mistakes is that of getting a bit carried away – aim to remove only a small amount of growth each time you trim. As long as you trim regularly, your shape will never get out of hand. Remember also that, especially if you are clipping freehand (without a framework underneath the plant), it is all too easy to lose track of the shape because it is impossible to see all angles at once. It can be a bit of a

Plants with attractive foliage add extra texture and interest, as shown here in this artful cloud creation.

shock when you stand back to admire your finished work and find that you have been a little more vigorous in some places than others. Like the artist in front of his easel, it pays to step back from the work at regular intervals so that you can monitor the overall effect as you go along.

Framework

Most topiary designs are easy to form using a framework or template. These help to make sure that your trimming is even and that there are

Don't forget

Always brush over the entire surface of the plant immediately after clipping. This will dislodge any pieces of leaf or stem that have settled into the foliage and stems of the plant. If this debris is left, it may harbour pests and diseases; even if no pest or disease is present, the decaying of accumulated dead foliage generates heat, causing sections of the plant to die at a later stage.

Once bitten by the topiary bug, you may find your collection of living art just keeps on growing…

no accidents, such as removing the wrong shoot. For simple shapes, such as a cone or pyramid, you can use bamboo canes as the template, although more complex shapes may need a moulded framework of wrought iron, chicken wire or a cane-and-wire structure. If you have the skill, you can make these structures yourself. Otherwise, it is possible to buy ready-made frames. Frames and templates don't find favour with the purists, but they are the perfect aid for someone who is tackling a topiary shape for the first time.

With more complicated shapes and figures, it is advisable to use a frame that is just smaller than the eventual size of the topiary. Position the frame over the plant and allow the shoots to grow until they reach the outer limits of the framework; then, once the growth emerges beyond the framework, trim it to make it bushy. Continue this process until the framework is no longer visible, but allow at least 5cm (2in) of growth beyond the frame; this will make sure the frame is totally hidden and reduces the risk of damage to pruners and trimmers when the shape is routinely pruned. Alternatively, remove the framework when the shape has been created and the formative pruning is almost finished, so that the last stages of formative pruning are 'freehand'. (Frames made from sections of metal bolted together are much easier to dismantle when they are no longer needed.)

Cone, spiral and globe shapes

A cone can be created fairly simply using a framework of bamboo poles and wire (*see* right). A spiral may take several years to produce as it has to be done in two stages (*see* opposite). With conifers and some evergreens, this process will need to be carried out early in the plant's life, before the growth becomes too woody, because pruning back into old, brown areas can spoil the whole effect if the plant is unable to generate new foliage from them. For both cones and spirals, it helps if you choose a plant that has a naturally upright habit.

The globe, or ball (*see* opposite), is one of the most popular shapes,

HOW TO make a cone

1 In late spring, after planting, prune back any long, vigorous shoots that start to dominate the shape and disrupt the overall balance of the plant. The aim is to create a neat, bushy habit in an approximate cone shape. Use secateurs at this stage to remove the unwanted shoots.

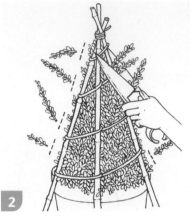

2 In the following spring, make a template using bamboo canes and wire. Place this over the plant and shake all of the branches to encourage the longer ones to emerge through the framework. Using sharp shears, clip over the plant, removing any growth that has emerged through the framework.

3 After the clipping is finished, remove the template and pinch out the top third of the growing point to encourage the plant to become even more bushy. This clipping and pinching will need to be repeated at least three to four times each year, depending on the plant used and its growth rate.

since it can be created without the need for gadgetry. The aim is to create a globe-shaped head to a plant growing on a short 'leg' or stem. *Laurus nobilis* (bay) is often grown like this to control its size and vigour. It is also easiest to prune once established.

make a spiral

Before you make a spiral, you need to create a cone (*see* opposite). Then, in late spring, wind a thick wire in a spiral shape from the base of the plant up to the uppermost tip. This is a useful cutting guide and will help you to turn your cone into a spiral.

1

2

3

Starting from the bottom of the plant, cut out a 'groove' of foliage along the length of the wire to create a channel. Continue this process over one to two seasons until a definite spiral has been achieved.

Trim the new growth around the wire regularly to maintain the plant's overall shape and to prevent foliage growing over the channel. The aim is to keep the spiral form as distinct as possible.

Carry out fine topiary pruning using a pair of topiary shears. To keep it looking perfect, clip in early summer and again at the end of summer, but you can get away with a single annual cut in late summer.

HOW TO make a globe

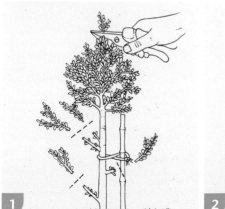

1

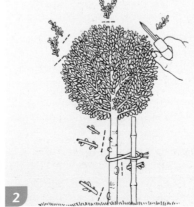

2

In the first year, tie the main stem of the standard to a cane to provide stability and prevent wind rock, and cut back by half the sideshoots growing from the lower sections of the stem. Trim back the main shoot in the top of the plant to encourage bushy growth.

The following spring, cut back the sideshoots that were pruned back by half in the previous year to create a clear stem. Once the plant has reached the required height, prune back the main lead shoot by one third, and trim back any sideshoots by half, to create a bushy 'head'.

Climbers and wall shrubs

With the average garden now being half the size of those of 50 years ago, gardeners today need to be more inventive than ever when it comes to finding ways to grow the plants they love. One particular aspect that is becoming ever more popular is vertical gardening, which is a real space saver.

Walls, fences, pyramids, gazebos and other upright structures provide an ideal opportunity for vertical gardening, with many different ways of supporting a range of climbers and wall shrubs. Any upright structure has the potential to be a support for tall or upright-growing plants, which can make an immediate visual impact. They also give a opportunity to hide, or at least disguise, some of their support structure; so these forms of natural camouflage are excellent for hiding those items in the garden that we need but would rather not see, such as dustbins, fuel tanks and compost bins.

Types of climber and wall shrub

Many plants that we think of as climbers in truth are not – most are just shrubs that happen to be trained to grow up a vertical support, be it a wall, fence, arbour, pergola or even an upright pole or post. As with other groups of plants, pruning can be made much easier by having a basic understanding of how these plants grow (and in some cases support themselves), when they flower, and so on.

Just looking at the plants will give an indication of how they grow and some guide as to how they are likely to react to pruning. True climbers have their own adaptations to help them support themselves, and many require only maintenance pruning and trimming; but they may need regular training, depending on their growth and vigour, to keep them growing in the desired direction. Most wall shrubs, however, will need to be trained and pruned more frequently, since they are often being encouraged to grow in a way that is not wholly natural to them.

The bright-yellow winter flowers of the scrambler *Jasminum nudiflorum*.

All these plants can be divided into four main groups, according to their growth habit: clingers, twiners, scramblers and wall shrubs.

Clingers

These plants have either aerial roots or sucker pads, which they use to cling to any support they can find (*see* opposite). Since they are self-supporting, they are ideal for growing against a wall or fence. Plants in this group include *Campsis radicans* (trumpet vine), *Hedera* (ivy – most types), *Hydrangea anomala* subsp. *petiolaris* (climbing hydrangea) and *Parthenocissus quinquefolia* (Virginia creeper).

Twiners

Some plants have rapidly growing shoots that twist and twine, coiling around any support they can reach. These include *Lonicera* (honeysuckle) and *Wisteria* (*see* page 75). With some other twiners, only a small section of their growth twists and twines; often it is a part of the leaf or stem that has been modified into 'tendrils', which grip a support. These plants include *Clematis* (*see* pages 79–81), *Passiflora* (passion flower), and *Vitis* (grape vine).

Scramblers

These are plants with rapidly growing stems that clamber through or over other plants, often relying on them for support. Many roses (*see* pages 84–93) have developed thorns to 'hook' onto plants as they scramble over them. Plants in this group include *Jasminum nudiflorum* (winter jasmine) and *Solanum crispum* (Chilean potato tree).

Wall shrubs

These plants are not strictly climbers, but they are either tender enough to require the protection of a wall or fence during winter, or they have brittle or unstable roots and need to be trained against a support. Plants in this group include *Ceanothus* and *Fremontodendron*.

Maintenance pruning and training

Left to their own devices, many climbers and wall shrubs produce masses of growth, which may smother neighbouring plants, and very few flowers. So, maintenance pruning and training is essential for most climbers and wall shrubs if you want to grow them well, but try to adopt a regime of guiding the plant's growth rather than trying to control it.

Most pruning is combined with training the growth from stems that have been attached to some kind of support. With self-supporting climbers, which will hold onto whatever is available, training is mostly based around getting the plant's shoots to grow in the direction you want them to.

With wall shrubs, maintenance training is focused on supporting the plant – otherwise it may keel over because it cannot support itself. Much of the training is geared towards keeping a framework of evenly spaced stems firmly attached to the support structure, with the actual manipulation of the stems carried out while they are supple enough to be positioned and tied into place.

The most difficult plants to train are usually those that are the most vigorous, simply because of the quantity and length of shoots being produced; these shoots soon become quite woody and lose their flexibility. Some types of wisteria,

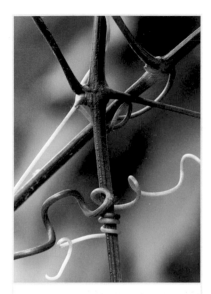

Twiners wrap their tendrils round any support, including canes, wires and the stems of other plants.

Lonicera (honeysuckle) and, particularly, *Fallopia baldschuanica* (Russian vine) can be difficult to train once established; often they are best left to grow freely and pruned only when they start to become invasive.

Clingers can attach themselves to just about anything. The aerial roots of *Hydrangea anomala* subsp. *petiolaris* (below right) stick themselves to brick with extraordinary tenacity. *Parthenocissus quinquefolia* (Virginia creeper, below left) hauls itself up a brick wall by sending out its sucker pads.

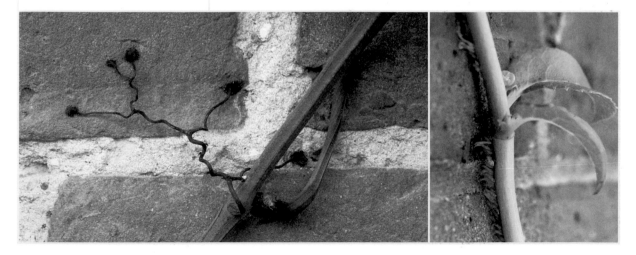

Formative pruning and training

Today, most climbing plants are purchased when they are actively growing. Some may also be in flower. Always trim off any dead or damaged shoots before planting your climber. Once planted, tie the remaining growth into position against its support structure. For the first year, the training will consist mainly of positioning and securing the strongest stems to create a balanced framework of well-spaced stems, each with an equal amount of room on the support structure. This is an ongoing task, as

the shoots need to be 'coaxed' into position while they are still soft and supple. You will need to check these new plants every two to three weeks, and tie in the extension growth until their own natural self-support system

(if applicable) starts to get to grips with the support structure they are intended to grow over. Time spent training shoots in these formative months will save a lot of heartache and unnecessary labour later.

The fast-growing honeysuckle *Lonicera periclymenum* 'Serotina'.

HOW TO prune a climber

In its first few years a climber should need very little pruning, but it does need to be trained and tied in to form a sound framework. Maintenance pruning is usually carried out on deciduous climbers while they are dormant, in summer for evergreens.

1 Immediately after planting, position and tie the selected stems into the support. Prune out any dead or damaged stems and remove any strong stems not needed as part of the plant's structural framework, to promote new growth. Throughout the growing season, regularly train into position the new extension growth.

2 The following spring, cut back all sideshoots close to the main stem, remove any frost-damaged growth, and cut out any shoots that are either overcrowded or not necessary to the shape. Tie the remaining shoots into position and space them out on the support structure to form the framework of the plant.

3 In subsequent years, cut back each of the strongest stems by up to one third to encourage new shoots to extend the structural framework of the plant. Cut back any thin shoots to two buds, and remove completely any unwanted stems. Tie in all the main stems and try to get the plants using their own support systems.

Wisteria is one of those plants that causes many gardeners a bit of grief. It can spend years producing masses of twining growth, with ne'er a flower in sight. To avoid this, buy one when it is in flower so you know it is of proven flowering capability (and, of course, so that you can be sure you're getting the colour you want).

Formative pruning

In the first spring, or immediately after planting, cut out any dead, damaged or diseased growth (frost-damaged shoot tips are quite common) and prune the tip of each shoot back to just above a strong, healthy bud.

In summer, as the young growths develop, train them into the support structure and space them out. Cut back any unwanted shoots to about 15cm (6in). In the spring of the second year, cut out any frost-damaged shoot tips, back to just above a strong, healthy bud. Remove any thin, weak shoots, and continue to train the strongest shoots into a horizontal position. Throughout the growing season, tie in the young growths as they develop. Prune back any excessively vigorous shoots to 15–20cm (6–8in) long, or train them into a horizontal position.

Getting wisteria to flower

Training can be every bit as important as pruning; when new shoots are trained into a horizontal position they tend to lose their vigour, which in turn encourages the formation of flower buds along their length. With pruning, the most effective way to encourage wisteria to produce more flowers regularly is to prune the plant twice each year. The first part of this two-staged pruning is done in late summer, when shoots not needed to extend the plant's territory are cut back to around 30cm (12in). The second (precision) pruning is done in late winter, when all of the shoots that were originally pruned in late summer are now cut back to form spurs consisting of two

All the hard work is worth it in the end!

or three strong buds, which carry the flowers. At the same time, cut back any secondary growths formed after the summer pruning to 15–20cm (6–8in), and any shoots damaged by frost or wind to a strong, healthy bud.

Don't forget

Many wisterias are propagated by grafting onto a rootstock, generally seedlings of *W. floribunda* or *W. sinensis*, and there will usually be a slight swelling low down on the plant's stem to show where the rootstock and top variety were joined together. If any shoots emerge from below this swelling, they are almost certainly suckers and must be removed as soon as they are noticed (*see* page 33).

Summer and winter pruning:
① In late summer, cut back all the current season's long lateral growths to 15–20cm (6–8in) from their point of origin. (There is no need to cut back to the bud as they will be pruned again later.) Shoots that are being retained should be tied into position until they start to twine and support themselves.
② In late winter, cut back all summer-pruned shoots to two or three strong buds; these will form the flower-bearing spurs. Cut back to 15–20cm (6–8in) any growths produced after the summer pruning (there will be a lot of these after a wet summer).

Pruning for fruit and flowers

In the first spring, or immediately after planting, cut out any dead, damaged or diseased growth, and prune the tip of each shoot back by about one third to encourage new growth. In summer, as the young growths develop, train them into the support structure and tie them in place; cut back any unwanted shoots by up to two thirds of their overall length.

In subsequent years, cut out any dead or damaged shoots in spring. At the same time, remove any clusters of berries that remain from the previous year. In midsummer, cut back all of the new growths to two or three leaf buds, and weak shoots back to one leaf bud.

In late winter, remove any very old, unproductive stems and thin out congested shoots to prevent overcrowding. Trim back any old fruit-bearing stalks when the berries have finished. Prune back any over-vigorous shoots that are not required or have spread beyond the plant's allocated space, and cut back any growths that are growing out too far from the support structure or spoil the overall balance of the plant.

Renovation pruning

Since most climbers and wall shrubs are given the benefit of a supporting structure, renovating overgrown and neglected specimens can be a major undertaking.

Trachelospermum jasminoides (star jasmine) flowers in summer, so it should be pruned in late winter or spring, depending on the risk of frost.

Wall-trained pyracanthas (here, *P.* 'Mohave') can be pruned in spring and again in late summer, shortening new growth to expose the berries.

First, you will need to decide if the plant concerned is worth trying to save – if the plant looks strong and healthy, it will probably cope with the challenge (and shock) of severe pruning. Plants that do not appear to be in good condition should be removed and replaced.

Neglected wall shrubs and, particularly, climbers often develop into a dense, tangled mess, with very little new extension growth and hardly any flowers, or lots of small ones. Renovation of a plant in this condition is no quick fix and may take several years, particularly for healthy but less vigorous plants, which are unable to cope with the shock of severe pruning. In such a case, it is advisable to renovate the plant in stages over a few seasons, rather than just cut it down. This makes life even more difficult, simply because for several years there will be a mixture of new, vigorous, replacement shoots and older growths, which will gradually be removed. Often, these new shoots can get tangled into the older growths, making later pruning difficult, and to avoid this it is worth pruning one section of the plant quite hard but leaving the rest. The following year prune another part, until gradually over several years the old shoots are replaced by new ones.

If this renovation works, the new shoots will be quite vigorous and will grow quickly, so they must be trained into the support structure as they grow to prevent them breaking or becoming damaged.

After pruning, apply a top-dressing of fertilizer, watering it in well. This will help to promote the rapid development of new shoots. However, ensure you do not over-feed the plant as regrowth may be too vigorous.

Routine pruning after renovation

After two or three years, as the plant recovers from this drastic pruning and starts to resume its normal growth pattern, it can be pruned as appropriate, depending on its growth habit and flowering season.

HOW TO renovate a climber

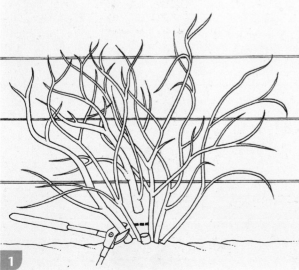

1

First, cut away any dead, damaged or diseased growth. In late winter or early spring, cut down to ground level a third or half of the stems, leaving the more vigorous ones. Feed with a balanced fertilizer and during the growing season, train the new strong stems into the support, tying them in at 30–45cm (12–18in) intervals as they grow.

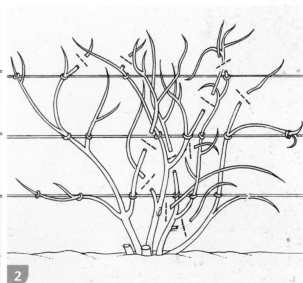

2

In the following winter or early spring, untie any of the new stems that are too close together, and retie them, evenly spaced, over the support. Cut down the tallest stems at the top of the supports and cut down the remaining stems to 30cm (12in) above ground level. Throughout summer, thin out overcrowded shoots and tie in new ones as they grow.

Evergreen climbers and wall shrubs

Many wall shrubs and some climbers are evergreen, and these are often chosen to hide eyesores in the garden or adorn a blank or uninteresting wall or fence all year round. Climbers such as the large-leaved *Hedera colchica* (Persian ivy) and the smaller-leaved *Hedera helix* (common ivy), with its coloured leaf forms, are perfect for this task.

As with other plants, the key to the timing of pruning evergreens lies in the reason for growing the plant – whether for its flowers or its fruits. Obviously, flowering is not a real issue with ivy, but *Trachelospermum jasminoides* (star jasmine) is grown for its fragrant flowers, which emerge through summer and into autumn.

For many evergreens, the best time to prune is in early summer, before the growth really gets going and to avoid new shoots being damaged by a late-spring frost.

Many evergreen climbers produce flowers on the previous year's wood. For those flowering in spring and early summer, such as *Clematis armandii*, the best time to prune is as the flowers start to fade. However, those that flower in summer and autumn, such as the honeysuckle *Lonicera henryi,* can be pruned either in late winter or spring (late-winter pruning can be a risk in colder areas because it may expose some stems that were protected under a layer of foliage, and these may suffer cold injury). Evergreen climbers are especially susceptible to wind chill.

The wall shrub *Pyracantha* (firethorn) is grown for its ornamental fruits and so it needs to be pruned thoughtfully. The best time to prune is in midsummer, trimming all of the new shoots back to two or three leaves – these will form flower-bearing spurs – and cutting back any thin, weak growths to just one leaf. Avoid cutting off stems that are carrying developing buds.

The variegated foliage of *Hedera canariensis* lightens a shady corner.

Most people when asked to name a climbing plant will think first of clematis. What they almost certainly do not know, however, is that if you grow a selection of the different clematis species and hybrids it is possible to have clematis in flower for every month of the year. Small wonder then that clematis is known as 'the queen of climbers'.

With these plants, pruning can be seen as a problem simply because there is such a vast range of shapes, sizes and colours, and if you have different plants capable of flowering at different times of the year obviously they cannot all be pruned at the same time and in the same way. However, despite the vast range of species and cultivars, they can be categorized into three basic groups, each of which has a recommended pruning regime. Group classification is based on the time of year the clematis would normally flower (see box, right).

The different flowering times of clematis determine when to prune.
① *C. orientalis* flowering in autumn.
② *C. armandii* in early spring.

If you kept the label when you buy the plant, you will know which group your plant belongs to (according to its flowering time). If you didn't keep the label, or you've inherited someone else's clematis, it is probably safest to wait and see when it flowers before running amok with the secateurs.

Formative pruning

Regardless of the group to which they belong, all newly planted young clematis benefit from hard pruning. Cut back all of the strong stems to a pair of healthy buds 30cm (12in) above ground level, and remove any dead or damaged growths and thin, weak shoots. Tie in the new shoots to their support at 20–30cm (8–12in)

Clematis pruning groups

GROUP 1
Early-flowering clematis

These are the relatively small-flowered clematis, including *C. alpina*, *C. armandii*, *C. cirrhosa*, *C. macropetala*, *C. montana*, and their cultivars.

Pruning Tidy after flowering.

GROUP 2
Summer-flowering clematis

These are the large-flowered clematis that flower between late spring and midsummer. They include *C.* 'Daniel Deronda', *C.* 'General Sikorski', *C.* 'Henryi', *C.* 'Josephine', *C.* 'Nelly Moser', *C.* 'Niobe', *C.* 'Rebecca' and *C.* 'Vyvyan Pennell'.

Pruning Light prune, late winter or early spring.

GROUP 3
Late-flowering clematis

These include *C. florida*, *C. orientalis*, *C. tangutica*, *C. texensis*, *C. viticella*, and their cultivars, and the large-flowered hybrids *C.* 'Bill MacKenzie', *C.* 'Cassis', *C.* 'Comtesse de Bouchaud', *C.* 'Duchess of Albany', *C.* 'Ernest Markham', *C.* 'Étoile Violette', *C.* 'Gipsy Queen', *C.* 'Jackmanii', *C.* 'Lambton Park', *C.* 'Perle d'Azur', *C.* 'Princess Diana', *C.* 'Purpurea Plena Elegans', *C.* 'Viennetta', *C.* 'Wisley'.

Pruning Hard prune, late winter or early spring.

Where to start with this Group 3 clematis? ① Before this clematis can be given its annual hard prune, the tangled top growth must be cut away from the support (in this case an obelisk). ② Cut back healthy stems to a strong pair of buds within 30cm (12in) of soil level. ③ With Group 2 clematis, cut back the stems to a strong pair of buds around 1m (3ft) above ground level.

intervals to prevent wind damage or accidental breakage.

In the second spring after planting, cut back all stems to a pair of buds 90cm (3ft) above ground level. Remove any weak or damaged growths. Where stems are competing, cut the weaker stems back to 30cm (12in) from the ground.

Pruning Group 1 clematis

These plants flower from midwinter to late spring on the previous season's growth. Many of these early-flowering clematis do not need maintenance pruning on an annual basis, but a number are quite vigorous and tend naturally to sprawl over everything around them. They are best pruned immediately after flowering; if they are pruned later much of the flower-bearing wood will be removed, giving a poor display the following spring.

In spring, soon after flowering, trim off the dead flowerheads (you can use hedge-cutting shears for this). With evergreen clematis, remove up to one third of the oldest stem to allow replacement shoots room to develop. Throughout summer, cut back any strong, vigorous shoots that start to spread beyond their allotted growing area.

Owing to their vigorous, sprawling nature, Group 1 clematis will need

some 'containment' pruning to keep them within their allotted space. This can be an ongoing procedure. With *C. armandii*, which often has sections of the old stems dying back, the best approach is to completely remove a proportion of the older stems in rotation; this will avoid congestion. After flowering, cut back to strong, young shoots or healthy buds.

Pruning Group 2 clematis

In early summer, these plants produce large, single, semi-double or double flowers on stems that emerge from the previous season's stems. Many plants in this group often produce a second flush of blooms on new shoots in late summer, although the cultivars with double flowers in

If pruned correctly in early spring (*see* left), a late-flowering clematis such as 'Madame Julia Correvon' will produce a large crop of flowers from midsummer to late autumn.

the first flush will often produce only single flowers in the second flush.

These plants are best pruned in early spring, just as the growth buds start to swell but before the new growth gets underway. Remove any dead, weak or damaged growth and cut back healthy stems by about one third of their total length to just above a strong pair of leaf buds, if possible around 1m (40in) above ground level. It is these buds that will produce the main flower display. Tie in the new shoots at 20–30cm (8–12in) intervals to train them into the support structure. To stagger pruning of the plant, cut some of the stems down to just two thirds of their total length.

To encourage the plant to produce a secondary flush of blooms, prune half of the shoots much harder in spring to encourage a more prominent later flush of flowers, and so extend the flowering season.

Pruning Group 3 clematis

These plants produce flowers in late summer and into autumn on the current season's stems. The best time to prune this group is in early spring, just as the buds start to swell, but before the new growth starts (*see* opposite). They can be cut down quite dramatically.

Pruning consists of cutting the plants down to a strong pair of buds within 30cm (12in) of soil level, with any thin, weak shoots being pruned back to a pair of buds as close to ground level as possible. When the new growth starts, thin out any congested areas by removing some of the overcrowded shoots, but careful handling is necessary as the new stems are brittle and easily snapped. As they grow, space the shoots evenly around the support structure and tie them in at regular intervals, until the tendrils take hold and the plant starts to support itself.

The three pruning groups:
① *C. alpina* (Group 1).
② *C.* 'H.F. Young' (Group 2).
③ *C. viticella* 'Polish Spirit' (Group 3).

New varieties and hybrids

A new generation of clematis is being raised by breeders. Much of the pruning for these is the same as outlined here – it depends on the flowering group the plant fits into – but the character of the plants is changing. Plant breeders are now introducing many varieties that are far less rampant, often reaching no more than 2–3m (6–10ft) in height, making them much more manageable for the gardener and considerably easier to reach and prune.

The other major change has been the plant breeders' success in introducing plants that produce flowers low down on the stems, rather than having the lower 1–1.5m (3–5ft) of the plant bearing only foliage.

Training climbers and wall shrubs

True climbers are at least partially self-supporting, so they often need little more than a bit of encouragement to scramble over another plant or structure – they will do the rest. However, in the early stages, you should give them a good start with some formative training. Wall shrubs need all the help they can get because they are shrubs, not climbers; support and constant tying in will be necessary to make sure they stay in place.

Climbers

You might think that a climber is a climber, but where plants are concerned it is seldom that simple, and it is easy to choose a plant with the wrong method of support for a particular site. For instance, climbers that use sucker pads to cling as they grow do not grip well onto wooden surfaces unless the wood is painted, so they need much more training until

they do finally take hold. (Climbers with aerial roots, on the other hand, seldom have any trouble, which is why ivy can get just about anywhere.)

Plants with tendrils will not coil around supports that are too thick or of a large diameter, and most wooden trellis is too thick for plants such as clematis. This means that the first shoots have to be tied in regularly, but

There are various types of support for climbers and wall shrubs.
① A tree is a good support for many climbing plants, such as this hydrangea.
② Climbers and wall shrubs can be tied into trellis fixed against the wall.
③ A wigwam in a container is ideal for a climber if there is not room for a trellis.
④ A strong fence can support a trained wall shrub, such as this ceanothus.

the second flush will cling to these older shoots for support, rather than the trellis itself. This may well be all right at the time, but when the plants are pruned and the older stems are removed the support for the younger stems goes too.

The tendrils of clematis have evolved from modified leaves. Ideally, their support should be no thicker than a pencil, so the plants can grip on easily. You often see clematis being trained around the downpipe from a roof gutter, with yards of string being used to try to make the plant climb. In that situation, the easiest option is to plant the climber as close to the downpipe as possible, then wrap sections of chicken wire around the pipe, leaving a 15cm (6in) cavity between the pipe and the wire and guiding the plant to grow in this cavity. The shoots will naturally grow out into the light, so they will cling to the wire (and soon disguise it). More sections of wire can be added as the plant gets taller.

With wisteria (*see* page 75) the most important part of training is to keep the stems separated where possible; otherwise they tend to twine around themselves and each other rather than around the support. Pruning is a twice-yearly task, while training is an ongoing process of tying and guiding shoots into the areas where you want them to grow.

Wall shrubs

Only a regime of regular pruning and training makes these plants grow against a wall or fence in a way that sometimes contradicts their natural growth habit. One of the easiest ways to train a wall shrub, keep it neat and tidy and have a good display of flowers, is to use some form of trellis or similar structure, with a large gauge of mesh; it must be strong enough to take the often considerable weight of the plant it is supporting.

Fasten the frame to the wall or fence, using spacers between the support and the structure it is attached to; a gap of 5–8cm (2–3in) between the two fixtures will leave enough space for the plant to grow into. Tie the plant to the trellis. As the wall shrub grows, it will naturally want to grow outwards, towards the light and away from the trellis; where this is the case, you just need to gently push the main stems back under the trellis frame to keep it against the fence or wall. As these main stems produce sideshoots, these will also grow out towards the light, and they can be trimmed back to four or five leaves (or buds if it is winter). These growths will often form flowering spurs. As the plant grows, the leaves will obscure most, if not all, of the trellis once the plant is established.

Regularly tie the plant back against the support structure to make it grow in the direction you would prefer. To get a better flowering performance out of most wall shrubs and climbers, try to train as many growths as possible into a horizontal position. This will cause a redistribution within the plant of natural hormones, which influence flower production in certain parts of the plant. Rather than getting long, erect shoots with a few clusters of large flowers at the top, bending stems down into a horizontal position and tying them into place will encourage the formation of flowers along the entire length of the shoot, giving far more flowers and a much better display (*see also* page 13).

Roses

It's easy to see why roses are so popular. As well as being beautiful, they are remarkably tough, adaptable and forgiving. They have a variety of growth habits: from bushy, miniature shrubs for growing in pots through to climbers, ramblers and ground-cover varieties with long, trailing stems. Most roses need regular pruning to ensure the best possible display.

As well as diversity of habit, roses have a surprisingly wide colour range that includes white, cream, yellow, orange, red, violet and every shade in between. In addition, some of the newer introductions are getting ever closer to a true blue-flowered rose.

Mind you, if roses have a fault it is that they can 'bite', or at least scratch. The one thing that is likely to put you off growing roses is the thought of sticking your hands into a plant bristling with thorns in order to

prune it. If this is the case, seek out one of the 'thornless' roses such as 'Perception', which has distinctive colouring and very few thorns, or the climber 'Zéphirine Drouhin', which is practically thornless.

Why roses need pruning

When left to their own devices, most roses will grow like many shrubs, producing new growth on existing branches, as well as some strong, vigorous shoots at soil level or close to the base of the plant. Once these shoots and stems have produced flowers and often fruits (hips), they will become progressively more gnarled and

Rosa 'Little White Pet' is a vigorous shrub rose with sprays of white flowers from summer to autumn. It tolerates hard pruning.

less flower productive and may eventually die. When we prune a rose, we are removing these old stems so that new, free-flowering ones replace them. The main benefits of pruning roses are to allow space for new stems to grow, create vigorous, healthy,

Rosa 'Princess Alexandra' has a bushy, upright habit and deep-pink, fragrant blooms that flower all summer.

Rose types

■ Miniature roses have compact growth and tiny flowers.

■ Cluster-flowered bush (floribunda) roses are upright or bushy in habit with dense clusters of semi-double or fully double flowers.

■ Large-flowered bush (hybrid tea) roses produce large flowers that have high, pointed petals in the centre of the bloom. They are carried in fewer numbers than those of cluster-flowered bush roses.

■ Shrub roses tend to have a more vigorous, less stiff habit than bush roses. The flowers may be single or double and many of them have a strong fragrance. They may flower in one brief but glorious flush in early to midsummer or repeat flower during the summer.

■ Species roses are often quite tall and usually carry single flowers in a single flush in early summer, followed by hips.

Some tall shrub roses, such as 'Graham Thomas', benefit from the support of a wall. They can be secured to horizontal wires strung between vine eyes.

well-shaped plants and encourage the maximum number of flowers. Pruning, if carried out correctly, can transform a rose from being just one of several attractive plants in the garden to becoming a magnificent, free-flowering display that steals the show in summer.

Basic rules for roses

There are many different types of rose, with widely ranging growth patterns, and the time of pruning differs according to the type of rose you are dealing with. However, there are some basic rules that can be followed and applied to most roses. As with pruning other types of plant, start with the four Ds (*see* page 19). When carrying out this process, always try to cut back into healthy wood. If the stem under the bark is brown or discoloured, keep pruning until you reach wood that is white or greenish white, as this is usually a sign of a healthy stem. The next stage is to remove any unwanted growths. This may include:

- overcrowded shoots
- crossing branches
- thin, weak shoots
- shoots with dead, withered hips.

In addition, you must keep an eye open for suckers (*see* page 86).

One of the main reasons that roses can have so much trouble with pests and diseases is because the centre of the plant becomes congested with thin, weak, twiggy shoots. So any pruning has to aim to keep the centre of the plant open and clear of crossing branches. If the branches are evenly spaced and allow a good flow of air through the plant, there is usually less of a health problem. To achieve this, try to prune down to an outward-facing bud to encourage growth away from the centre of the plant. Make the cut 6mm (¼in) above a bud (*see* pages 28–9).

Avoid the scratch

Whenever you are handling roses, it makes sense to wear gloves. But there is something else that will help you avoid injury from these thorny plants, and that is to bear in mind that all roses originate from scrambling plants. This means that their thorns evolved not as a weapon for lacerating the hapless gardener, but for the purpose of hooking themselves onto other plants for support. For this reason, rose thorns are curved and tend to point down the stem, not up it.

When you need to get at a particular stem, follow it from the top downwards (or from the growing point backwards), so that your hand travels in the same direction as the thorns' curve and not against the sharp tips. Cut the stem off and pull it away from the plant with your other hand.

Suckers

One of the biggest problems with roses are suckers (*see* page 33), and in these plants they must be dealt with as soon as they appear.

Most modern roses have been grafted onto the rootstock of a species (wild) rose in order to increase their vigour and longevity. Since the species rose is naturally more vigorous than the grafted rose, the species will attempt to reclaim itself by sending out its own shoots at any opportunity. These unwanted shoots are called 'suckers'. They can either emerge from the soil in the area around the base of the plant or from the base of the plant itself, just below the graft union where the variety and rootstock are joined together. Suckers can be recognized by their leaves, which are often smaller and a slightly different colour from those of the grafted rose.

The best way to remove suckers is to rip or pull them out. Cutting them off the parent plant often results in more suckers forming, particularly if the shoot has not been removed flush to the stem or branch where it emerged.

In late winter or early spring, set to work on the four Ds, removing dead, damaged, diseased and dying wood. For thick stems, like the one here, use a pruning saw.

If suckers are not removed, they will very soon get their way – the species rose will eventually replace the grafted cultivar. Never cut them off at ground level, as this will only encourage more growth; instead, trace them to their point of origin on the roots and pull them off carefully at the root (*see* below). Standard roses, which are top-grafted, may produce suckers on their stems: pinch them out or cut them back to the stem.

The most common reason for suckers appearing is when the plant has been subjected to hard pruning, but there are also other causes. If the roots have been damaged in some way, most commonly by hoeing too deeply, a natural response as part of the healing process is for the plant to form suckers to replace the damaged shoots.

Timing

When to prune roses depends on the type you're growing and the effect you want to achieve. It also depends on when you plant: roses planted in the dormant season are

pruned on planting; container-grown roses planted in the growing season should not be pruned until their first spring.

Winter pruning

Most modern bedding roses are pruned at this time. Although it has always been called winter pruning, in reality we are talking about late winter and early spring, often just as the roses are showing signs of new growth for the coming season. The timing of the appearance of the new growth can often vary by several weeks from one year to another, and also depends on your location and the prevailing weather conditions. Wait until you can see the buds on the top half of the shoots starting to swell (and when the weather is not freezing) before you start to prune.

If you prune too early, and then the weather becomes mild and the plants

The white, cluster-flowered bush rose 'Iceberg' (foreground) should be cut back to 30cm (12in) above the ground in late winter or early spring. This retains the rose's attractive rounded habit and improves flowering.

come into growth early, this growth may be damaged later by frosts. This will delay flowering, and the plants cannot really be pruned again. Also, if the roses bleed lots of sap after pruning and then the temperature drops, some stems may split.

The problem with pruning later in spring, when the plants have produced lots of top growth, is that you cause the plant to waste energy. The plants will take time to recover and produce more new shoots, delaying flower development by as much as three weeks.

Summer pruning

This usually means dead-heading (*see* page 88) to promote the production of more flowers, and it is carried out during the flowering season with modern roses. With species roses such as *Rosa rugosa* or *R. moyesii* (grown for attractive hips that last well into winter), it is unusual to dead-head these plants at all, although young plants may have their hips removed during the first season after planting to help them establish more quickly.

Views on how to dead-head roses are often divided. One school of thought says that you should cut off the dead flowers with a section of stem (as if you were cutting roses for flower arranging): this encourages the plants to produce new stems from lower down. Another believes that just removing the dead flower and the small stalk that attaches it to the plant is better, as it retains more leaves that are producing food to support the plant. Each rose is different and if a variety has a vigorous habit it is worth just removing the flowers to stop the plant from getting too tall; if a plant has a weak habit, it is better to cut further down when dead-heading to encourage new, stronger shoots to grow.

Climbing and rambling roses respond well to being pruned in late summer or early autumn, when old, non-productive shoots can be removed completely.

Autumn pruning

Bush roses with a tall, upright habit, especially those growing in exposed, windy areas, are very vulnerable to a problem called 'wind rock', particularly in autumn.

As the name suggests, the force of the wind levers against the long stems, causing the roots to loosen. If, in extreme cases, the roots break and dry out, the rose may die. Where this is a risk, it is worth cutting the growth of the plant down to half of its overall height (called 'topping') to reduce its wind resistance. Then prune the plant in the conventional way in the following spring.

Relay pruning

This method of pruning is used where roses are grown together in ornamental rose beds (often of a single variety). Alternate plants are pruned quite hard, with the remainder pruned in the usual way. The hard pruning will delay flowering by several weeks, so that the flowering period is staggered. The lightly pruned plants will be at their peak just as the severely

pruned plants are starting to flower, extending the overall flowering period within the bed.

Pruning the different types of rose

Roses as a group of plants contain a mind-boggling number of hybrids and cultivars, in addition to the species (wild) roses. For the purposes of pruning, though, you need to know only the type of rose you are dealing with.

Bush roses

The bush roses can be divided into two groups: the large-flowered type, sometimes called the 'hybrid tea', and the cluster-flowered type, also known as floribunda.

As with the pruning of other woody plants, start by completely removing any dead, diseased or damaged shoots. The growth that is left will give you some indication of

Formative pruning of bush roses

In winter, immediately after planting, remove any thin, weak, damaged or crossing stems, then prune each of the strongest, thickest shoots down to 8–10cm (3–4in) above ground level. Cut the shoots to an outward-facing bud to encourage an open centre.

what you have to work with. Remove any thin, spindly, weak stems or shoots (with most of these roses any shoots thinner than a pencil are too small to leave). Cut out any shoots that are crossing the centre of the plant, to give the plant a goblet-shaped, open centre with a perimeter of strong stems.

With well-established plants, remove old stumps from clusters of branches that have built up over previous years. These may be thick enough to require a pruning saw or loppers. Again, discard the thinnest, weakest stems, and cut

HOW TO prune a mature bush rose

1 In late winter, remove any dead, damaged, diseased or dying wood. Cut out any weak, spindly growths and any shoots growing across the centre of the plant. This improves the shape of the bush and prevents congestion.

2 Prune the remaining shoots of large-flowered roses to 15–20cm (6–8in) above ground level. Prune the main stems of cluster-flowered roses down to 25–30cm (10–12in) and all the sideshoots back by about half their original length.

During the growing season, dead-head the plants to remove the spent blooms as they appear, which helps to prolong flowering.

back the stems to be retained to form the main framework of the plant. Large-flowered roses (hybrid teas) are pruned more severely than cluster-flowered roses (floribundas) due to their increased vigour. As a general rule, hybrid teas can be cut back to 15–20cm (6–8in) and floribundas to 30cm (12in) above the ground. Avoid the temptation to be too lenient with them, since this leads to a build up of old, gnarled stems and bushes that grow far too tall to be ornamental – often carrying their flowers sparsely and above head height.

Miniature and patio roses

These are small plants, often with thin, spindly shoots that become overcrowded, and there is a tendency for some of the shoots to die back. For this reason, pruning consists of thinning out overcrowded shoots (which reduces the die-back problem) and cutting the shoots back by one third of their overall length. You can also reduce the length of any over-vigorous shoots

that throw the whole plant out of balance. Dead-heading will consist of lightly trimming the plants with small shears to remove the large numbers of small, dead flowers after each flush has finished.

Shrub roses

This term covers a large and varied group of roses, usually larger and more branched than the bush roses. They include species (wild) roses, old garden roses, modern shrub roses and ground-cover roses. Most flower on wood that is two or more

years old, and many will flower freely for a number of years without any formal pruning.

With species roses, each year cut out any dead, dying, diseased or damaged wood as a matter of course. The pruning of the live wood usually consists of taking out a few of the oldest stems as low to the ground as possible to allow room for replacement shoots. The best approach is to completely remove two or three of the oldest stems each year, so that over three or four years all of the growth is gradually renewed. Lightly tip the remaining shoots to remove any soft growths that may be damaged by frost or injury caused as they whip about in the wind.

Alba, damask and moss roses are better pruned immediately after

Standard roses

These are normal bush, miniature, patio, rambler or ground-cover roses that are grown on an extended rootstock to add an extra dimension to the plant. Bush and ground-cover roses tend to be budded or grafted onto the rootstock stem about 1–1.2m (3–4ft) above soil level. Miniature and patio roses are often budded or grafted onto the rootstock stem about 60–75cm (24–30in) above the ground. Rambling roses are often budded or grafted onto a stem at a height of 1.5–2m (5–6ft), or even higher, so that the long stems can trail down, making an 'umbrella' shape – these are known as weeping standard roses.

The variety on the top of the rootstock is referred to as the 'head' of the standard, and the pruning will be the same as for those plants budded or grafted at ground level. So the 'head' on a floribunda rose grown as a standard will be pruned in the same way as a floribunda rose growing down at soil level. The main difference in pruning is in the timing of the operation. Standards are much more likely to suffer from wind damage during the winter months, so they are often pruned in late autumn to reduce their wind resistance.

flowering, as this gives the plant a chance to channel its energy into the development of new stems. With established plants, two or three of the oldest stems can be cut down low (even to ground level) to encourage new replacement stems. After these have been removed, prune the remaining stems lightly by trimming off the end quarter of the main shoots and removing about half of the growth on each sideshoot to leave as much flower-bearing wood as possible.

The main exceptions within this group are plants such as *Rosa rugosa*, *R. moyesii* and their respective hybrids, which are valued for their attractive display of hips. These roses should be pruned in late winter, after the hips have gone.

Rosa 'Glore de Dijon'is a highly fragrant climbing tea rose. Prune in autumn, after flowering has finished; dead-head and tie in new growth throughout the growing season.

Often, pruning will consist of cutting out two or three of the oldest stems to encourage new replacement shoots and tipping any sideshoots by removing the end third.

Climbing roses

Climbing roses tend to produce erect growth on stiff stems, and many will flower more than once in a growing season. Some are vigorous mutations ('sports') of bush forms of rose – these can easily be spotted since the name starts with 'Climbing', such as *Rosa* 'Climbing Iceberg' or *R.* 'Climbing Peace'.

In the first year after planting, climbing roses are usually left alone, although it's worth giving them a light trim to remove damaged shoots. This is particularly important for climbing sports of bush roses, because severe pruning may result in this type of rose reverting to its original bush form. Although little or no pruning is carried out in the first year, some training can be done as soon as the new shoots become long enough to handle, usually when they reach 30–45cm (12–18in).

For older types of climber, and most of the climbing 'sports', the best flowering performance is achieved by training the shoots out along horizontal supports to get a distribution of flower buds along the entire length of the shoot rather than just on the end third. Many modern climbing roses will naturally produce flowers just above ground level, so

The long stems of climbing and rambling roses need tying in to a support to protect them from wind damage.

Climber or rambler?

The difference between these two types of rose is not as clear-cut as it once was. This is because many new varieties have been developed as a result of interbreeding between the two groups, and to add to the confusion some modern shrub roses are grown and trained as climbers or wall shrubs.

It is worth pointing out that any plant that is considered to be a 'true' climber is one that can support itself – with tendrils, twining stems or sucker pads – which probably means that there is no such thing as a 'climbing' rose. They might be better described as wall shrubs. Because these roses are not truly self-supporting, training is just as important as pruning if they are to flower and grow well.

the shoots are often trained out in a fan formation on a wall or fence (*see* opposite), or 'spirally' around an upright support such as a pergola.

Most climbing roses grow and flower well for many years with nothing other than a tidy-up to remove dead or damaged growth in autumn, just as flowering finishes. However, some flowers may need to

HOW TO prune and train a mature climbing rose

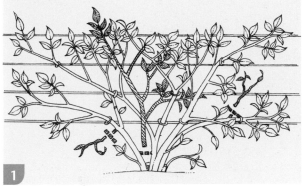

1 Prune out unwanted stems in autumn before training and tying in the new season's stems. Start by removing any dead, damaged, dying or diseased wood. Cut out any thin, weak, spindly growth, and thin out any congested shoots from the centre of the plant.

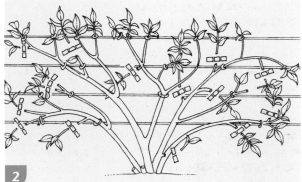

2 Cut out any crossing stems and train the remaining stems into the wire. To the right and left of the centre of the plant, you can bend the stems a little to meet the wire. This horizontal training will encourage more flowers (*see* page 13). You will, of course, have to keep some stems growing vertically to maintain the overall balance of the plant.

be sacrificed, simply because in a mild autumn varieties such as *Rosa* 'Mermaid' will not shed their leaves and often keep flowering until midwinter if grown in a sheltered site.

In autumn, the strongest main shoots that make up the framework of the plant can be left unpruned, unless they become too long and vigorous for the space they have been allocated. Reduce any overlarge shoots by at least one third to encourage them to form sideshoots, or remove them completely to make room for the new season's growth, which can be trained into the spaces. This process of renewal pruning ensures that, over several years, the oldest, least productive growth is gradually replaced by younger, more vigorous stems. Any sideshoots on the older main stems can be cut back to about 10cm (4in). Remove completely any young shoots that cannot be trained into a suitable position.

Rambling roses

Rambling roses are usually more vigorous than climbing roses. They produce long, lax growth. They usually flower only once each year, although some may produce smaller, secondary flushes of flower. Most of their flowers are borne on wood formed in the previous year, usually on small laterals (sideshoots) developed on strong, vigorous stems. Since most of these plants produce a single flush of flowers in midsummer, the best time to prune them is soon after they have flowered, usually in late summer.

You can leave rambling roses alone and they will flower for years, but true ramblers are closely related to 'wild' roses and if left alone they will swamp a corner of the garden or the

side of a house with a mass of long, whippy shoots, usually covered in large thorns. The flowers will be well out of reach and you will risk life and limb if you try to get near them. If you prune out the old shoots you don't want or need, and train in the

Rosa 'François Juranville' is a rambler with clusters of salmon-pink flowers in summer. Prune after flowering.

new ones to provide space for each stem, you will be well rewarded.

Ramblers produce lots of new shoots from the base of the stems each year. This results in overcrowding, leading to poor air flow around the shoots, which is made even worse if they are growing against a wall or fence. The warmer conditions and still air are perfect for encouraging fungal diseases, as well as aphids and other pests.

Immediately after planting, remove all dead, damaged and diseased wood. Also prune out any thin, weak growths and cut back the remaining stems to about 45cm (18in) above soil level. As the new vigorous shoots grow, spread them out over the area the plant is intended to cover, training them as close to a horizontal position as possible. These shoots are much easier to train while they are still soft and supple.

After the third year, when the plant is well established, prune more severely to maintain a planned framework and create space for new growth. After removing all dead, damaged and diseased wood, cut out a quarter of the total number of stems, targeting the oldest shoots that will no longer produce flowers. These will be replaced with vigorous new stems and strong, healthy, two-year-old growths. Once all these stems have been tied in, cut back any sideshoots to two or three buds. These will form flower-bearing spurs.

Low-growing roses of trailing habit (ground-cover type)

There are two divisions within this group. First, there is the modern shrub type such as the *Rosa* 'Flower Carpet' series, and county roses such as *R.* 'Avon', *R.* 'Kent' and *R.* 'Surrey'. These need pruning only to keep

Tie in the long, young shoots of climbers and ramblers and shorten sideshoots to two or three buds.

them growing within their allotted space, and to remove the shoot tips to encourage them to branch and cover the ground more quickly.

The other group contains the creeping 'rambler' type, including *R.* 'Grouse' and *R.* 'Nozomi'. These are much more vigorous but usually flower only once a year. They are pruned immediately after flowering, cutting out some of the old, flower-bearing shoots completely.

Renovation pruning

Roses are very resilient and most can tolerate quite extreme pruning, especially if they are healthy, well-fed plants. This is just as well, because many, if left unpruned for several years, will become a matted, tangled mess of growth and produce fewer, much smaller flowers than normal – even the flower colour can become poor. To make matters worse, the whole plant will also be much more prone to pest and disease problems.

The more vigorous types of rose, particularly the ramblers, can cope well with all of their stems being pruned back hard, and will usually respond by sending up long, trailing shoots to replace those that have been removed. However, you may need to spray to control mildew as these soft, sappy growths frequently suffer from this fungal disease.

Most climbing roses will need to be pruned in stages, usually over two consecutive winters, as the old growths are gradually replaced by new ones. With the climbing versions of bush roses (sports), renovation pruning is much more risky; sometimes these plants respond well, but on other occasions they have been known to revert to their bush form as a result of the shock created by this extreme pruning.

Exceptions

Although for most roses renovation pruning is a means of recovery to get them back to their former glory, with a few roses it can be the only feasible way to prune them. Climbers and ramblers that are grown up into trees or through large shrubs cannot be pruned in a more conventional way, so they must be renovation pruned every seven to ten years. In effect, the plant is cut back very hard, often to within 50–75cm (20–30in) of ground level, and a whole new generation of growth is then trained to replace the old.

HOW TO renovate a rose

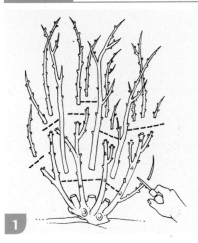

1

In autumn, ideally before leaf fall, cut out all dead, dying, diseased and damaged wood. In late winter, cut down to ground level half of the remaining stems (take away the oldest, thickest ones first). Shorten the rest by half and cut back the sideshoots to three or four buds.

2

In summer, if large amounts of growth have been produced, thin out overcrowded shoots by removing every third one. Remove any sucker growths by pulling them off at their point of origin (see page 86). Make sure you also remove any dormant buds at the base of the sucker.

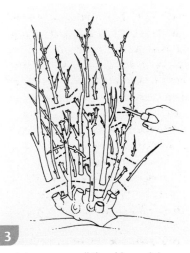

3

In winter, remove all the old remaining stems that were not cut out last winter, as well as any diseased, damaged or unwanted new shoots, to prevent overcrowding. Shorten the rest by half and cut back to three or four buds any sideshoots that formed on strong, vigorous stems produced during the growing season.

4

In summer, cut back hard any 'blind' shoots – that is, ones that do not have signs of a flower bud at their tip or have no obvious growing point. Shortening the blind shoot will stimulate a lower bud into growth, and so the shoot may go on to produce flowers later in the season. The most likely cause of blind shoots is frost damage to the shoot tip.

Soft fruits

The term 'soft fruits' covers a range of fruits that are generally borne either on bush plants (as in the case of black-, red- and whitecurrants, gooseberries, blueberries and more exotic plants such as goji berries) or on plants with a rambling or trailing habit (as with blackberries, loganberries and raspberries). The ramblers are known as cane fruits. Grape vines and kiwi fruit, both climbers, are also classified as soft fruits.

The pruning regime

With the pruning and training of soft fruits, the primary aim is of course to produce the maximum crop each year, while at the same time keeping the plants strong and healthy. The plants must also be kept accessible so that you can get at the fruit (which in practice means keeping them tidy). To achieve this, the pruning and training regime must be fairly strict and regular, and it is this that can seem a bit daunting when you first start growing soft fruit. In fact, it isn't really

Gooseberry 'Whinham's Industry' is a reliable cropper, producing fruit on short 'spurs' on the main branch framework.

HOW TO prune fruit bushes that flower on the previous season's wood

This is the pruning regime for free-standing plants that produce fruits on the previous season's wood. In particular it applies to blackcurrants and jostaberries. (For clarity, leaves are not shown.)

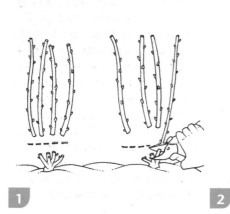

1

2

During the first spring (just as the buds start to swell), or soon after planting, cut down all stems to one healthy bud just above soil level. This will speed establishment. The following winter, cut out any damaged branches, and prune any thin, weak or small shoots back to just above ground level. Thin out any strong shoots that are growing too closely together.

In the following and subsequent summers, soon after harvesting, cut out the oldest fruit-bearing stems as close to ground level as possible, or to just above a strong new shoot low down. Remove any short, thin, weak, damaged or diseased shoots. Some winter pruning may be required after leaf fall, when it is easier to make a judgement about the structure and balance of the plant.

Blackcurrant plants should be spaced about 1.5m (5ft) apart. Some varieties, such as 'Boskoop Giant' (shown here) can grow up to 1.5m (5ft) tall.

complicated, but you do have to be systematic about it.

The aim is to achieve the right balance between fruiting, the production of new growth, and shape (for control and accessibility). As with most gardening, experience is usually the best teacher. So if you find your plants are producing a huge amount of new growth (but, later in the season, very little fruit), it is likely that you were somewhat overzealous with the secateurs. If they produce hardly any new growth at all, you were probably not assertive enough to spur the plant into growth – you might get plenty of fruit this year but there won't be enough new growth to produce a good crop the next. Once you develop a feel for how much needs to be cut back when, you'll find growing soft fruits surprisingly straightforward.

Bush fruits

These are usually grown as 'free-standing' plants (with no supports). Gooseberries, redcurrants and whitecurrants are mostly grown on a short stem – a 'leg' – or as standards or half-standards to keep the fruit above the ground (especially useful for cultivars that have a lax, weeping habit, such as the gooseberry). You can instead grow many bush fruits as cordons (see training trees, pages 42–3), but this is a complicated method that is not worth the trouble unless space is very limited.

Blackcurrants and jostaberries

These plants produce fruits on wood made the previous year, so pruning is geared towards producing vigorous

Where space is at a premium you can train some bush fruits into cordons. Here, the redcurrant 'Stanza' is trained against a wall as a double cordon.

new shoots to replace those that have finished cropping. Ideally, you should prune by removing stems close to ground level to encourage the plant to produce long, vigorous shoots from the base.

Once the plants are established, use a system of renewal pruning, cutting back approximately a third of the stems to ground level each year. Do this in late summer after picking the fruit: this will ensure that the plant's energies are directed into the development of the following year's fruit-bearing stems.

As the bushes age, you may find that fewer shoots are produced at low level. If this happens, prune out old wood as low as possible, just above a young shoot, and always

remove or cut back any thin, weak or diseased shoots.

Gooseberries, redcurrants and whitecurrants

Unlike blackcurrants, these plants produce fruits on short spurs, which are developed by pruning back the lateral branches (sideshoots). Most of the fruits are produced on shoots that are two or three years old; shoots that are four or more years old produce very few. Gooseberries and currants are usually grown on a short stem or 'leg' to keep the fruits from touching the ground.

The best time to carry out formative pruning of currants and gooseberries is late winter or early spring, before growth begins. Remove any low branches to produce a short, clear stem ('leg'), and shorten the remaining shoots by half; the aim is to create a framework of up to six branches. In the following winter, cut back all the new growth by half to form the framework of main branches. Prune back to a single bud any shoots that are growing into the centre of the bush or in a downward direction; even though these shoots are unwanted, these remaining buds may develop into fruit-bearing spurs.

In subsequent years, aim to create and maintain a wine-glass shape. Remove low-growing, overcrowded and crossing shoots to keep the centre of the bush reasonably open and clear of growth. This helps the fruits ripen and makes picking easier, as well as allowing good air circulation through the plant.

A properly pruned, established plant should consist of nine to twelve shoots, ranging from one to three years of age. Prune out all four-year-old shoots, thinning out some of the new growth. Cut out any old non-fruiting shoots to encourage strong young shoots to grow into the available space. Sideshoots can be cut back to finger length in summer to form fruiting spurs.

Standard and half-standard gooseberries

The cultivars of gooseberries grown as standards or half-standards are the same as those grown as bushes, but they are grafted onto a 'leg' or stem: about 1.2m (4ft) above soil level for a standard, 60–90cm (2–3ft) for a half-standard. The 'leg' is usually a three-year-old stem of *Ribes odoratum* or *R. divaricatum*, both of which make a very good rootstock and should be about 1cm (½in) thick at the point where the cultivar is grafted onto the stem. When planted in their permanent cropping position, standards must be staked, as the stem alone is not strong enough to support the weight of the cropping cultivar unaided.

These plants are pruned in exactly the same way and at the same time as the bush forms, but watch out for 'sucker' growths which may appear on the rootstock: these should be removed as soon as they are seen (*see* page 33).

HOW TO prune fruit bushes with a stem or 'leg'

This pruning regime applies to plants that produce fruits on short spurs and whose natural habit make them suitable for growing on a short stem or 'leg'. In particular it is the regime for pruning gooseberries, redcurrants and whitecurrants (right).

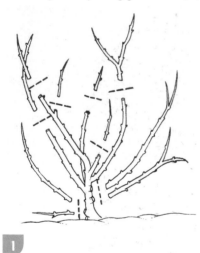

1 In the first winter (or immediately after planting), remove sideshoots lower than 20cm (8in) above ground level to form the main stem or 'leg' of the bush. Select up to six stems to form a framework, and prune them back to half their original length, cutting to an outward-facing bud. Remove all other stems, including any broken or damaged ones or any with visible signs of disease. In the following winter, cut back all the new growth by half.

2 In late winter or early spring of subsequent years, remove any dead, damaged, diseased, weak or low-growing shoots. Reduce overcrowded or crossing stems to about 2cm (1in) long. Cut out old, unproductive shoots, and shorten the rest by about a quarter. In later years, cut back the leaders each winter by about a quarter of the amount they grew the previous season. Fruiting and age will slow the leaders' growth until they need only light tipping or nothing at all. In summer, shorten sideshoots to finger length.

Red- and whitecurrants, like this variety 'White Grape', are less rampant than blackcurrants. Leave 120–150cm (4–5ft) between plants.

Quite aside from the significant health benefits that the fruit is reputed to offer, blueberry plants are worth growing for their ornamental value alone.

Blueberries

Blueberries are one of the 'superfoods' that everyone talks about now, but they are also delightful ornamental shrubs with white bell flowers in spring and superb autumn leaf colour. To grow well, they *must* have an acid soil – with a pH of between 4.5 and 5.5 – and for this reason they are often grown in containers. For effective pollination, you need to grow more than one plant.

The fruits are borne on wood that is two or three years old, so pruning usually consists of gradually replacing the oldest or least productive stems.

Formative pruning (*see* right) usually involves cutting back any dead, damaged or weak shoots in order to promote strong, vigorous growth; otherwise newly planted bushes need very little pruning for the first few years. After this, a system of renewal pruning should be carried out in midwinter, after leaf fall. Having cut out any thin, weak or diseased shoots, cut out about 20 per cent of the shoots (selecting the oldest or least productive first). Stems should be cut down to ground level or pruned low to a stronger, younger lateral stem. This 20 per cent reduction should be done each year: over a period of four or five years all the shoots will have been replaced.

Pruning of blueberries. In winter or immediately after planting or potting, remove any dead or damaged shoots and cut back any weak shoots by half their length to a healthy bud. Repeat this process the following winter. If the plants produce flowers in these first two years, dead-head them to prevent any fruits forming and to channel all the plant's energy into new growth. Thereafter, prune out a few stems to the base each year to encourage new wood, but avoid removing more than one in four of the main stems. Remove weak, horizontal or crossing growth.

HOW TO prune a suckering shrub (Goji berries)

In the first spring or immediately after planting, start by pruning back any dead or damaged wood. Next, cut back the main stems to about 45cm (18in) above ground level, and remove any thin, weak shoots at the base. In the second year, remove any remaining stems that were cut down to 45cm (18in) in the previous year, and cut out any thin, weak shoots.

In late winter or early spring of subsequent years, cut the main stems back by about a third, shorten the lateral shoots by about half, and cut out any thin, weak growths. Cutting out one or two of the oldest, non-productive stems encourages new shoots to emerge at soil level, as well as controlling the overall size of the plant. In the summer or autumn, dig up any suckers that are too far from the plant.

Support for cane fruits

The main thing about cane fruits is that they can get into an awful tangle, so before you plant them and begin formative pruning, ensure that you have a support that will help you keep them in order. The easiest and most commonly used method is to erect a system of evenly spaced horizontal wires secured to strong upright stakes. As a general rule, the longer the horizontal wire, the greater the crop. Allow at least 23cm (9in) between each wire, so that each stem can be trained along a wire without becoming tangled with stems above or below it.

Goji berries

Like blueberries, Goji berries are now considered to be one of the 'superfoods'. The goji berry plant makes a large suckering shrub up to 3m (10ft) high and 2.5m (8ft) across, and can become invasive if it likes its spot. The plants usually flower in early summer, and often continue throughout the summer; they can go on producing fruits until the first frosts.

Although these plants require only a little pruning, harder pruning will keep the bush shaped and under control. (They are very tolerant of severe pruning and can regrow from old wood if renovated.) Pruning the main stems and branches will keep the plant shorter and thicker. It will also increase flower and fruit production – as well as improving

the flavour of the fruits (important, given that this is probably why you're growing your own in the first place).

Goji berry plants can be grown as hedges, which should be cut back hard in spring. To keep them in shape you may want to trim them again in early summer, but this does reduce berry production.

Cane fruits

These plants can be divided into two groups:
- Group 1 – those with upright, stiff, erect growth (mainly raspberries, but also some forms of blackberry that have erect stems and only a semi-trailing habit).
- Group 2 – those with long, lax, trailing growth (such as blackberries, boysenberries, loganberries and tayberries).

Group 1 cane fruits

The main member of this group – raspberries – can be further divided into two categories: summer fruiting and autumn fruiting.

Summer-fruiting plants produce canes in one growing season, and in the following season the same canes produce fruit-bearing sideshoots. Autumn-fruiting raspberries are sometimes described as 'ever-bearing' because they often give two crops per season: one in mid- to late summer (produced on the previous season's canes), and one in autumn (produced on the current season's growth).

In the first spring, or immediately after planting, prune all new raspberry canes down low – to one bud above soil level. This will encourage strong, vigorous shoots to emerge from the base of the plant and also promote new root growth, helping the plants to establish.

Summer-fruiting raspberries

Regular pruning is essential to keep these plants cropping. This is because the fruits are produced on shoots that developed in the previous

season, and also because they are naturally suckering plants. If they are left unpruned, new shoots (suckers) appear each year further and further away from the original plant. Don't be tempted to keep these if they are thin and weak: they will produce poor-quality fruits.

The best time to prune summer-fruiting raspberries is immediately after harvesting. This will direct all the plant's energy into developing new canes for next year's crop. Any canes that bore fruits should be removed because they will not produce fruits a second time.

After pruning, tie the remaining canes into the support structure, removing any very short canes completely; also remove any that emerge outside your designated row area. This is a pruning routine that is easy to get into, but check in winter that any old canes have not been overlooked.

The new shoots are usually light brown or, with some cultivars, green with red thorns. The two-year-old wood is often grey, with the oldest wood at the base of these stems being dark brown with greyish, peeling bark.

Autumn-fruiting raspberries

These varieties produce fruits on branches formed in the current growing season. For better establishment, do not allow the plants to produce any fruits during

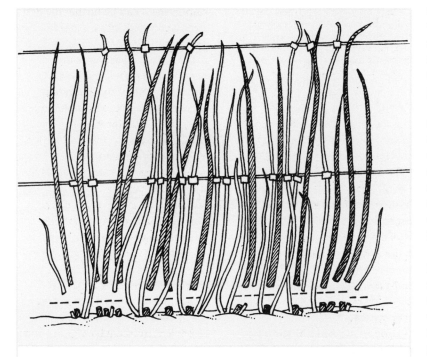

Routine pruning of summer-fruiting raspberries. Soon after harvesting finishes, remove all the old canes that have borne fruit, cutting them right down to soil level. Thin out any overcrowded new shoots, leaving one cane for every 10cm (4in) of row, and prune out all shoots that are less than 90cm (3ft) high. Tie in the remaining new shoots, spacing them evenly along the support. After leaf fall, look for any tall canes that reach well above the top wire and tie the tips to the top wire for support before reducing them in height so they are just 15cm (6in) above the top wire.

HOW TO prune and train autumn-fruiting raspberries

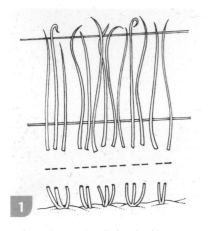

1

In late winter or just before bud burst, cut all canes to 7.5cm (3in) above ground level. If you want early summer fruits, leave some of the previous year's canes, removing 15cm (6in) from the growing tip, and cut them out after they fruit.

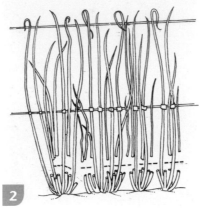

2

In early summer, thin out the new shoots to 7.5–10cm (3–4in) apart. Remove any surplus canes to avoid overcrowding, and take out all shoots less than 1m (3ft) high. Tie in the remaining new shoots, which will fruit in autumn.

their first year. In summer, remove any thin, weak or distorted shoots, and loosely tie the remaining shoots into the support.

Routine pruning of these consists of cutting all growth to 7.5cm (3in) from the ground in late winter or just before bud burst.

The autumn-fruiting plants are very versatile. With the right pruning regime you can get them to produce a crop in summer as well as in autumn: in late winter, when you would traditionally cut all the canes down, leave some behind; these canes will crop in summer while still allowing the traditionally pruned canes to push through and crop in autumn. Plenty of room needs to be left for the new canes, however, or the autumn crop will be reduced, so leave no more than a quarter of the old canes.

Group 2 cane fruits

The most commonly grown of this group is the blackberry.

Blackberries are easy to grow, but their very lax habit (which defines Group 2 cane fruits) means that training is extremely important. The other thing to know about them is that they are rampant, and if you don't keep on top of them they very soon become an impossibly tangled mess (which – given the spines – can be painful as well as frustrating to sort out).

You can grow blackberries against a fence or shed, if you have one, but you need at least 1.8m (6ft) of horizontal space for even the most compact varieties. Others, especially some of the older varieties, can reach 9m (30ft) or more!

In the first spring, or immediately after planting new canes, prune the

strongest, thickest stems back to within 25–30cm (10–12in) of soil level, and cut down to soil level any thin, weak shoots. This will encourage the development of strong, vigorous shoots from the base. As the shoots grow, train them along wires. If any grow to exceed 2m (6ft) in length, remove the end 15cm (6in): this will encourage the formation of lateral shoots, which will bear the fruits.

With routine pruning you are aiming to remove old stems that have already borne fruits, make room for new fruiting canes, and encourage the development of strong, vigorous shoots to replace those that will be removed after fruiting. To get the maximum benefit from their growth habit, these plants are usually pruned very soon after the berries have been picked, with the old canes being cut down to soil level.

Pruning and training should be carried out at the same time. With training you are aiming to keep the old and new shoots apart: you can then see at a glance which shoots need to be removed after fruiting and which ones should be retained for next year's crop. Training the canes along evenly spaced horizontal wires makes the berries much easier to pick and also minimizes the transfer of pests and diseases from old canes to new.

Creating an 'open fan' The open-fan arrangement is ideal for growing these vigorous plants in areas where space is at a premium. This involves training the canes to be kept for fruiting to the left and right of the centre of the plant, depending on which side of the centre they are growing from, and tying in the new canes, as they form, to the 'central parting' between the two sections of older cane.

The fruiting canes are evenly spaced and tied along horizontal wires to allow lateral shoots to form, while the new canes are loosely tied into a central column in the area between the older canes. This method prevents the new and old growths merging into a tangled mass, which often results in the new shoots being damaged as the older ones are removed.

The blackberry 'Loch Ness' is justly popular: it is not as lax as some varieties, and it's thornless – making it altogether easier to manage than the more usual kinds.

HOW TO prune Group 2 cane fruits (fan method)

(For clarity, leaves are not shown.)

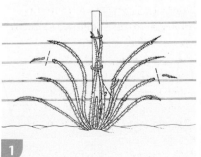

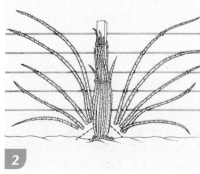

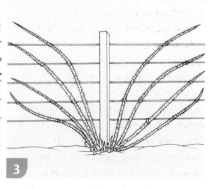

1

In spring, remove any shoot tips that show signs of pests, disease, damage, or die-back. Train the best canes along wire supports about 30cm (12in) apart to form a fan. As new canes grow from the base, tie them loosely to the post in the centre.

2

Soon after harvest, cut out all the old canes of the fan close to ground level. If left, they will usually become too rampant and not fruit well, so it is better to replace them with the new stems from the central bundle each year.

3

Select the strongest of the new canes and train them into a new fan. Avoid overcrowding, and cut out any thin, weak or diseased canes. As before, leave a central 'parting' between the two wings of the fan for the next generation of canes.

Vines

In the past, the word 'vine' was almost synonymous with grapes, but changes in climate and tastes, and the increased availability of other more exotic fruit, mean than other plants now come into this category – either because they have a similar growth habit or because they can be trained in a similar way to grapes. (This is why kiwi fruit is now often included in plant catalogues under 'vines'.)

There are many training and pruning methods used for vines, but

---

HOW TO train cordon vines up and across a pergola

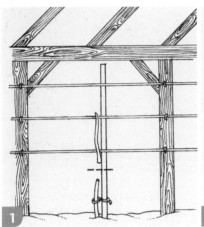

1

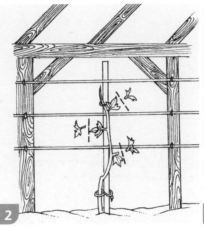

2

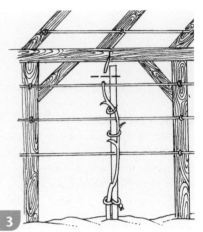

3

After planting in late autumn or early winter, shorten the stem of the young vine by about two thirds of its length. Cut to just above a strong bud.

During the growing season, select one strong shoot to form the main stem or 'rod', and train it vertically on a cane. Remove any tendrils and cut any sideshoots emerging from it to one leaf.

In winter, prune back the main stem to a strong, healthy bud, as near as possible to the overhead training support. Fix wires on the overhead supports, ready for training the vine horizontally next year.

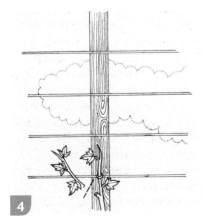

4

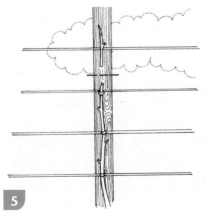

5

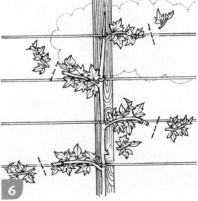

6

(Overhead horizontal support of pergola, viewed from below.) As new growth begins in spring, select one strong shoot for the horizontal rod and tie it in to prevent its being damaged by the wind.

(Viewed from below.) As the selected stem grows, continue to tie it in horizontally along the support structure. In late autumn or early winter, cut back the end third of the stem.

(Viewed from below.) Allow a strong lateral shoot to form every 30cm (12in). Cut these to five or six leaves in summer, and remove surplus shoots. Cut any that form on the vertical stem to one leaf.

for most gardeners the most practical way is to train a vine as a climber on a wall or fence, particularly where garden space is limited. The most common pruning methods used for vines fall into two basic categories:

■ the cordon (or rod-and-spur) method, which involves having a stem or branch framework that lasts many years and has fruit-bearing shoots (spurs) developing from it;

■ the renewal method: a framework of branches is replaced (renewed) over a period of one to three years.

Cordon method

With this, probably the most versatile method of training, you create a framework on which permanent fruiting spurs are formed. It can be either a single- or double-rod system (the 'rod' is the main stem). The rods can be trained vertically or horizontally – or both (vertically up the wall of a house for several metres before being trained horizontally – either overhead on a structure such as a pergola or the roof of a conservatory – or along the wall).

Keep flower trusses to a minimum for maximum crops of juicy grapes.

Grape vines produce fruits on the current season's growth, which means that spring and summer pruning is necessary to limit the number of flower trusses that are allowed to form and mature from each spur system. If you don't do this the quality of the crop will suffer. Also restrict vegetative growth by pruning new growth from the sideshoots, otherwise the foliage canopy will restrict light to the fruits and hinder ripening.

For formative pruning, train one stem up to at least 2m (7ft) so that the grapes will hang above head height; on a house wall you may need to train it above the height of ground floor windows, usually about 3m (10ft). Once the required height has been reached, train the main stem horizontally until it reaches the desired length; this growth will form the permanent framework with fruit-bearing shoots (spurs) trained at

HOW TO maintain cordon vines

(Overhead horizontal support, viewed from below.)

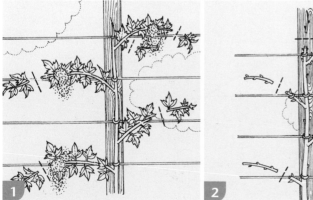

Each spring, allow one lateral to form every 30cm (12in). Prune these to two leaves beyond the flower cluster, and any sideshoots to one leaf. Prune laterals that fail to flower back to five or six leaves.

In winter, cut back the laterals to two strong buds. Reduce the new growth on the leader by half until it is the desired length, and from then on cut it back to two buds each winter.

right angles to the main horizontal stem on an annual basis.

Once a fruiting framework has been created, allow each spur to produce two shoots. Let the stronger shoot on each spur grow, and pinch back the weaker one to two leaves. Also prune back to a single leaf any other shoots as soon as they start to grow. This lateral shoot from the spur on the rod will provide the grapes; when the flower trusses develop in the summer, keep only the best, removing all but one truss per lateral.

The laterals should be stopped at two leaves beyond each selected flower truss. Any laterals that are not bearing flowers should be cut back to five leaves, and sublaterals (shoots growing from the laterals) should be cut back to a single leaf.

Renewal method

This is used for grape varieties and other fruit-bearing climbers that will not produce enough fruiting shoots from the basal buds left by spur pruning. Longer lengths of ripened wood, or canes, are kept for the following season, and from these fruit-bearing laterals emerge.

The 'double Guyot system' is the most commonly used renewal method for grapes grown outdoors. It involves the pruning and training of shoots emerging from the short, original main stem to create two horizontal rods from which fruiting shoots are trained vertically on a

A more informal approach to training: simply allow the vine to scramble up anything it pleases, tying in as it goes.

system of supporting wires. The training is more labour intensive than the cordon method, but it is very useful for producing large quantities of good-quality grapes in a small area.

In the first winter after planting, cut the vine stem back to 15cm (6in) above ground level. (If the grape has been grafted onto a rootstock, though, this should be to 15cm (6in) above the swollen graft union.) Then prune and train the vine as shown opposite.

Repeat the process each year. However, for the first few seasons, mimimize stress to the young plant by restricting the number of flowers each fruiting shoot produces. As the plant matures, and its 'leg' thickens, it can bear more flower trusses.

Vitis 'Brandt' is a dual-purpose variety with modest-sized bunches of sweet dessert grapes and foliage with superb autumn colour.

train vines by double Guyot renewal method

In the first winter after planting, cut the vine stem to about 15cm (6in) above ground level (just below the bottom training wire).

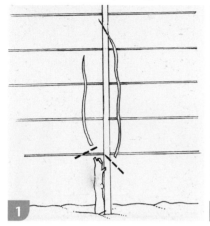

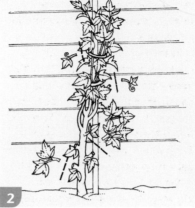

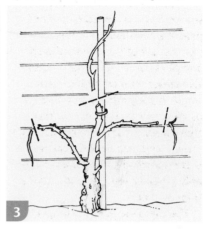

In early summer, select two strong shoots and tie them to the vertical cane support. Remove any other shoots that develop. In late autumn or early winter, cut the two shoots just above a bud, 7.5cm (3in) from the point at which they are growing from the main stem.

As new growth begins in the following spring, select three strong shoots growing from the top of the leg; remove all the others. Tie these shoots loosely to the upright cane. Remove any tendrils that form, and cut back to one leaf any other shoots growing from the selected stems.

After leaf fall, tie the two strongest stems to the bottom wire and cut them back to 60cm (2ft) long. Prune the remaining third shoot to 7.5cm (3in), just above a bud. Allow the horizontal rods to produce three fruiting shoots; rub out any others.

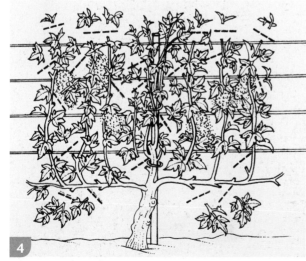

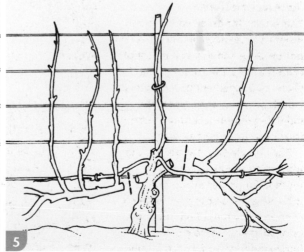

From now on, vertically train three shoots from each rod each summer. At first, pinch them out at the third wire and let only one cluster of flowers set fruit on each vertical shoot. In later years, grow them longer and allow one cluster every 30cm (12in). (Any that grow above the top wire should be tipped at two leaves above it and any sideshoots removed.) Allow three new shoots to grow from the central stem.

In winter, remove the rods and vertical shoots that fruited in the summer. Bring down the two strongest of the three stems that you allowed to grow in the centre to replace them. These will produce new fruiting shoots in the coming growing season. Cut back the weakest central stem. The base will produce new shoots, from which you will once again selcet three to become the replacement rods for the following year.

Kiwi fruit

This is a vigorous climber with twining stems. It produces fruits on one-year-old wood or at the bases of the new shoots, although it can take a new plant up to five years before it starts to flower regularly. Male and female flowers are borne on separate plants, and in order to get a successful crop it is essential to have both male and female plants growing close together. However, there is now a self-pollinating cultivar, 'Jenny', and it is possible to buy a female plant with a section of male plant grafted onto it.

In most gardens, the plants are best trained as espaliers on horizontal

HOW TO prune and train kiwi fruit

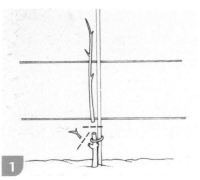

During the winter, or soon after planting, cut the main stem back to about 30cm (12in) high and remove any other shoots that are competing with it.

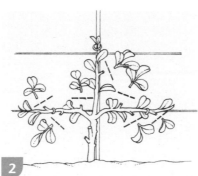

As the new growth starts, select the three strongest shoots. Tie one to the cane to keep as the main stem, and train the other two horizontally along the lowest wires. Remove any other shoots.

Actinidia deliciosa 'Bruno', seen here, is a bountiful cropper suitable for growing at home; 'Heyward' flowers later, so is more reliable if you suffer late frosts. Both need pollinators.

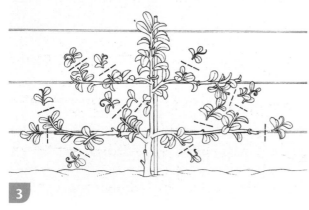

In summer, prune the horizontal laterals back to 90cm (3ft). Allow sideshoots to develop on them at 50cm (20in) intervals, and cut these back to five leaves to form fruiting spurs. If suitable laterals appear, train them horizontally on the next wire.

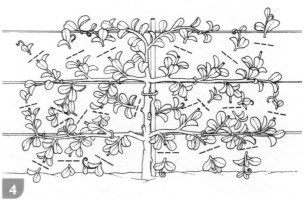

Late the following spring, cut the main stem back to the wire above the topmost branches, and select the strongest shoots to form the next tier. On these, allow fruiting shoots to form and prune them as on the lowest laterals. Continue each year until the desired size is reached.

Kiwi plants can become very large, but regular pruning will keep them in check and ensure a good fruit harvest.

wires set about 30–45cm (12–18in) apart. Any 'winter' pruning should be carried out in late winter or early spring after the risk of severe frost has passed; although pruning this late may result in some bleeding of the pruning cuts, this does not appear to harm the plant. It is important that these plants are not allowed to twine when grown as espaliers; they must be tied to support canes to keep the stems straight. The aim is to create a number of tiers or layers of horizontal stems that will carry fruiting spurs along them.

They need frequent tying in (as they grow very rapidly), but it is important to do this only after the new shoot has hardened enough not to break when it is bent into

position and secured. These plants need to be pruned both during the growing season and in the dormant season to control their vigorous

habit and to encourage flowers and fruits to form; the aim is to continually replace shoots that are older than three or four years.

HOW TO maintain kiwi fruit

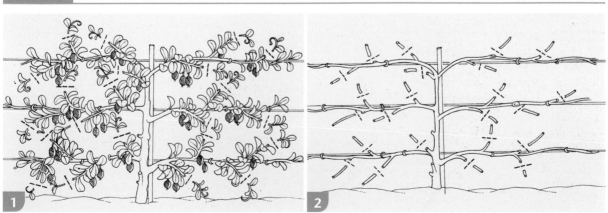

1 In summer, shorten sideshoots to five leaves beyond the fruit. Cut back any bare, unproductive lengths of growth to five leaves, and any new shoots growing around the fruiting spurs to seven leaves.

2 In midwinter, prune fruiting shoots to two or three buds beyond the point where the last fruit was borne. On older vines, cut back three-year-old fruiting shoots to a dormant bud or new shoot at the base.

Top fruit

Top fruit – fruits produced on a tree – usually conjure up images of large orchards. But, with the increasing availability of self-fertile varieties (those that can produce a crop without needing a pollinating partner), and rootstocks that produce smaller, more productive plants, you don't need acres of space to grow your own fruit. A patio will do. However, training and pruning does have a significant effect on the quality and quantity of your crops.

A Victoria plum tree grown as a bush in the garden border.

Different methods of pruning and training designed to increase fruit-bearing and to work with the natural growth pattern of the plant, have all made fruit easier to grow than ever before. The 'scaled-down' trees grown in the average garden also have a particular advantage over their grander cousins, in that pest and disease control – as well as picking and pruning – is so much easier.

Some tree fruits are 'tip-bearing', meaning that they carry most of their fruit on the tips of shoots grown in the previous season. These are best grown as standard, half-standard, or bush forms, because on each shoot

there are areas of bare, unproductive wood. 'Spur-bearing' types carry their fruits on short branches or 'spurs', on shoots that are at least two years old, and the fruits are usually borne in clusters. Most apples and pears are spur bearing, but a few are tip bearing and may need to be pruned in a slightly different way.

Grafted plants

When you buy a plant you often get two separate but closely related plants grafted together (the usual exceptions are figs and mulberries). The rootstocks are selected for their capacity to produce lots of fruit

(especially while the tree is still young); their habit (dwarfing rootstocks that produce smaller trees are usually preferred); and their resistance to certain pests and diseases.

Many of these qualities can be passed from the rootstock into the cultivated variety when the two plants are grafted together, so the gardener can have a good idea of what size and type of tree to expect from a cultivar joined to a named rootstock. Obviously, these qualities will also have an effect on how plants are pruned and how they respond to pruning, so it always helps to know what rootstock has been used to produce your tree.

You can create a superb garden feature using trained fruit trees, then enjoy the fruits of your labours – literally!

Ways of growing tree fruits

Tree fruits can be grown by two different methods: as free-standing or trained plants.

Free-standing trees include bushes, dwarf pyramids, standards and half-standards. They are not trained against a wall, fence or other structure, although a stake is important, especially for trees grown on dwarfing rootstocks, which need extra support to keep them stable.

Trained trees include cordons, espaliers and fans. These are trees grown with the aid of a support, such as a wall, fence or wires, with the branches trained into a particular shape along a flat surface. This method involves specialist pruning and is used to produce a large quantity of fruits in a small area. Such training is especially useful for trees that are not fully hardy, as a wall or fence provides some shelter and protection.

Apples

The most commonly grown top fruit is the apple (*Malus domestica*), with the majority being eating varieties. There are also a few dual-purpose cultivars (used for both eating and cooking), such as 'Blenheim Orange', 'Bountiful' and 'Charles Ross'. These are popular with gardeners who have very little space for growing fruit, or who want to limit the number of trees they need to look after.

Bush forms

The form of apple most often seen in the domestic garden is the bush. This is grown on a short, clear stem, with an open centre to the branch

system to aid ripening and make picking easier. Most apple varieties will grow very well as a bush, especially on a less vigorous rootstock, which means the fruits can be picked without the need for a ladder.

Most young trees have some formative pruning as part of their culture when in the nursery. This will usually have created a clear stem, about 75cm (30in) high, and a main stem or leader with three to four evenly spaced lateral branches

HOW TO prune bush-form apples

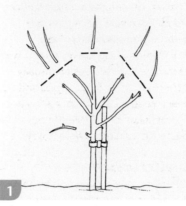

1 In late autumn or early winter, prune the main leader back to 25cm (10in), just above a bud. Cut back the side branch leaders by half, cutting to an outward-facing bud.

2 In late summer, cut back to three leaves any lateral shoots that are not required for branch leaders. Do not prune the branch leaders or main leader, unless they have been damaged.

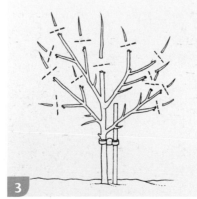

3 In late autumn or early winter, again cut the main leader back to 25cm (10in). Prune newly formed branch leaders back by half their length, and those formed in the first year by one third of their new growth, always to an outward-facing bud.

4 In late summer, cut back the lateral shoots to three leaves, and any sublaterals emerging from these lateral shoots to one leaf. Leave uncut any shoots shorter than 20cm (8in).

radiating out from it. These laterals will form the basis of the permanent branch framework. Within three to four years of planting, the formative pruning should have created a framework of eight to ten main branches, as well as several lateral branches. The centre of the tree should be open to allow a good air flow and good light penetration.

When pruning established bushes, the aim is to maintain a balance between forming new healthy

growth and producing good-quality fruits on a regular basis. When the structural framework is established, only winter pruning is necessary in subsequent years. The level of pruning will vary from year to year,

Apple 'Calville Blanc d'Hiver', a spur-bearing tree, is a dual-purpose variety for cooking and eating.

Tip-bearing apples. In winter, remove one in four of the oldest fruit-bearing branches to make room for the next generation. Thin out crowding in the centre of the bush and remove any water shoots that developed after the previous year's pruning. Lightly prune only the tips of leading branches.

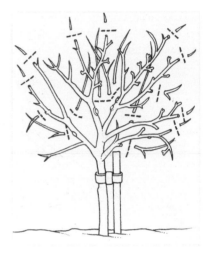

HOW TO prune spur-bearing apples

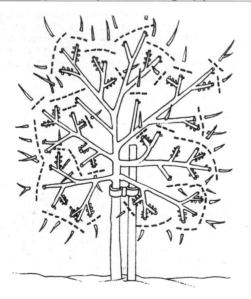

1

During the winter while the tree is dormant, cut back the end third of each branch leader. Prune back new laterals on the rest of the framework to five buds, to encourage more fruiting spurs to form.

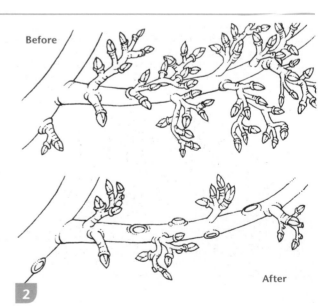

Before

After

2

Thin out any overcrowded spur systems. Remove old, weak spurs and any that develop on the underside of the main branches. Aim for one spur cluster every 10–13cm (4–5in) along the branches.

depending on the previous season and the type and amount of growth that was made; there is always more pruning to do after a wet growing season. The fruiting habit of the tree will also have a bearing on how the tree is pruned – spur-bearing apples need regular spur thinning, while tip-bearing ones are pruned using a renewal technique.

Trained apple trees

There are several different ways to grow apples as trained trees. They are sometimes grown as cordons, but the most popular form is the espalier. This is created by training the tree into a series of two or more tiers of horizontal branches, which are set about 40cm (16in) apart and grown in opposite pairs at right

angles to the main stem (*see* below). Espalier trees are usually sold part-trained, with at least one completed tier of horizontal branches, but often with two trained and a third partially formed.

Initial training concentrates on getting the framework of branches growing horizontally at regular intervals. Each year the main stem is

---

HOW TO form an espalier

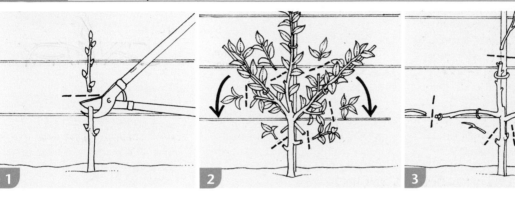

1. Start with an unbranched stem or 'maiden whip'. In the first winter, shorten it to just above a wire at about 45cm (18in). As new growth begins, select two strong shoots to form the first branches.

2. In summer, train the shoots on canes set at 45 degrees, and cut back to five buds any shoots growing from them. Remove unwanted shoots from the central stem. At the end of summer, lower the branches.

3. Next winter, cut back the central leader to the wire immediately above the new tier of branches. Prune the branches back by a third. Once the espalier has filled the space, simply remove all the current season's extension growth each winter.

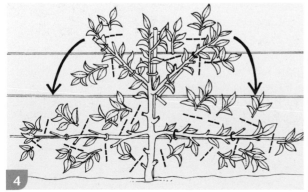

4. Next summer, select another two shoots to form the next tier. Tie them to canes and prune and lower them as in the first summer. Repeat this each year until you have the number of branches you want, then remove the leader in summer.

5. In midsummer, as the bases of the new shoots from the branch framework become woody, prune them back to three buds. Prune weak growth back to a single bud. In winter, thin out the spur systems (*see* spur pruning, page 110.)

pruned to the nearest horizontal wire, ideally where three healthy buds are located close together, to form the next tier of branches and the new main stem, which will be trained vertically as it grows. The two shoots that will form the next tier of branches are trained onto canes set at a 45-degree angle as they grow, then bent down to horizontal at the end of the growing season. This process is repeated annually until the desired number of tiers has been achieved.

A cordon is basically a vertical 'pole' which has the fruit growing on short twiggy 'spurs' along its length. Cordons can be grown upright or trained at a 45-degree angle along canes or wires. They can be planted individually where space is limited, or several can be positioned 45cm (18in) apart to form a 'hedge'.

To form the cordon, cut out the tip of the main stem in late July every year to the height that you find best

'Winston' is an apple variety that is reliable cropper – easy to grow and resistant to most diseases.

for maintenance and harvesting. Working along the main stem, cut back the current year's shoots on each spur to one leaf beyond the cluster of leaves where the new growth leaves the spur, or just beyond a developing fruit. Check the main stem for any emerging shoots that have not yet formed a spur and cut them back to within 23cm (9in) of the trunk. These will form new fruiting spurs.

Pears

The pruning requirements for pears are very similar to those for apples, although pears will cope with much harder pruning as they tend to be much more vigorous than most apple cultivars. Spur production is also much more abundant on pears, especially once they have started to produce fruit on a regular basis, so a major part of pruning with many pear cultivars is spur thinning to maintain the size and quality of the fruits.

There are a number of different ways to grow pears. The espalier form is particularly favoured in cold or exposed sites where some shelter and protection is needed, particularly at blossom time. (The training of espalier pears is the same as for apples – *see* page 111.) They can also be grown as bushes or standards, but one of the the most popular forms is the dwarf pyramid.

Dwarf pyramid

The dwarf pyramid shape and structure is based on a main central stem with a framework of branches radiating out from it; the branches becoming progressively shorter towards the top. The aim is to create

a Christmas-tree shape, which will maximize space between the fruiting branches: this will allow light into the tree to aid fruit ripening and to make fruit picking easier.

Dwarf pyramid trees can be bought part-trained with at least the lower tier of branches already formed, but it is more common to buy a 'feathered maiden' tree, which has a single main stem (central leader) and about five lateral shoots of various lengths radiating out from it. After planting, or during the first winter, the main stem and any lateral shoots are shortened, and any weak or damaged shoots are trimmed or removed.

During the early years of the tree's life, aim to build a sturdy stem and strong framework of branches capable of carrying fruit-bearing spurs. To encourage good establishment, any blossom that forms in the first two to three years should be removed from the central leader and lateral branches.

Once you have your established framework, prune the tree twice a year. Summer pruning is done to control the vigour of the shoots and direct as much of the tree's energies as possible into developing fruit-bearing growth. Winter pruning is used to control the overall height, size and shape of the tree; any spur thinning required is also carried out in winter. Pruning to maintain the size and shape of established trees may need to be done in both winter and summer once the tree has reached the desired size.

Root pruning (*see* page 116) should be carried out if the tree is becoming too large for its allotted space.

prune a dwarf pyramid pear tree

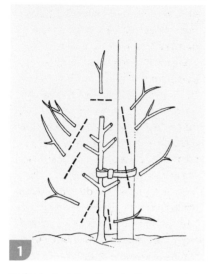

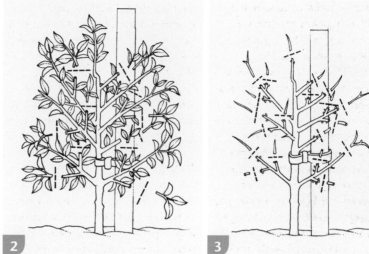

1

2

3

In the first winter after planting, prune back the central leader to a strong, healthy bud about 60–75cm (24–30in) above soil level. Remove any unwanted laterals and prune the remaining laterals to within 15cm (6in) of the main stem.

During the first summer, prune back any new lateral shoots to five buds. Cut any sublaterals emerging from the laterals to three leaves.

After leaf fall in the second winter, cut back all of the current season's growth to leave about 25cm (10in) of growth.

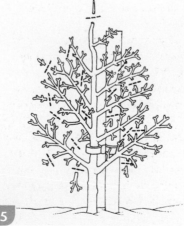

4

5

In the second and subsequent summers, prune back the new lateral growths to five buds; prune back any sublaterals to three leaves. (Each season this pruning will include the tiers of branches formed in previous seasons, as well as the new tier of branches formed during the growing season.)

In the winter, after leaf fall, prune the top of the central leader, leaving about five buds on the current season's growth. Prune out sections of overcrowded fruiting spurs to remove the oldest, least productive shoots. Some sections of older branches may need to be removed to create space for new shoots to emerge.

The russet-coloured, late fruiting pear 'Olivier de Serres' is a reliable variety that makes an excellent standard or pyramid.

Bark ringing fruit trees

One way to slow down apple and pear trees that are growing too vigorously and not fruiting very well is to use a technique called 'bark ringing'. This involves removing a strip of bark from the trunk in late spring, thereby restricting the flow of sap (and nutrients) to the top of the tree and limiting the supply of foodstuffs to the roots. It is a technique that needs to be used with care (and not on stone fruits such as plums and cherries).

Bark ringing can be performed only once a year, and great care must be taken to keep the cuts covered, as infection by fungal or bacterial disease in this region can be fatal. The aim is to remove a narrow strip (ring) of bark from around the stem of the tree, exposing the wood beneath. This ring should be wide enough to restrict sap flow, but not so wide that it is unable to heal within a year. (A longer healing time may result in damage to the tree.)

If possible, try to make the bark rings about 75cm (30in) above soil level. This is a comfortable height at which to work and to be able to inspect the cuts to see how well they are healing.

This process can be repeated each year if required, but if you do it again, you should never remove the bark from exactly the same place twice. Always make any new cuts just above or just below the cuts that you have made in previous years.

HOW TO bark ring a tree

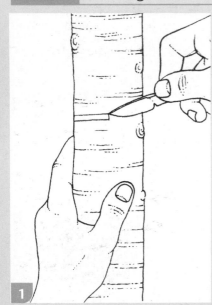

1 Make two horizontal, parallel cuts, between 3mm (⅛in) and 1cm (½in) apart, depending on the size of the tree, all the way around the stem.

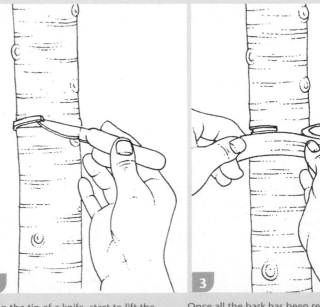

2 Using the tip of a knife, start to lift the bark out from between the two cuts. Pull this strip of bark strip away from the tree to leave a clear 'ring' of bark-free trunk.

3 Once all the bark has been removed, cover the open wound with a strip of electrician's insulation tape. This will keep water out and reduce the risk of infection.

Plums

Plum trees produce fruits on two-year-old wood, at the base of one-year-old wood, on fruiting spurs. Most plum varieties tend to produce lax growth with a spreading habit, often giving a weeping appearance, which means they may become too large for the smaller modern garden. Most are therefore grown in columnar form (which you can buy formatively pruned under various names such as Minarette or Ballerina) or as a pyramid with a central stem (similar to pears).

HOW TO prune a columnar plum tree

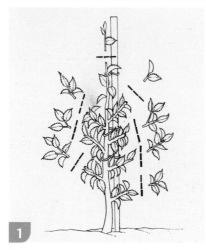
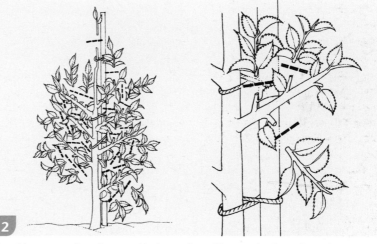

1 As new growth starts each spring and summer, allow the central leader to grow to about 45cm (18in) long; then prune it back to 30cm (12in). With vigorous trees this may need to be repeated several times each year.

2 By midsummer, when the new sideshoots (laterals) emerging from the main stem have produced plenty of extension growth, cut them back to six leaves. Cut back new growth on the leader again through the summer if necessary. Once sublaterals have grown to about 15cm (6in) long (*see* detail right) cut them back to a single leaf.

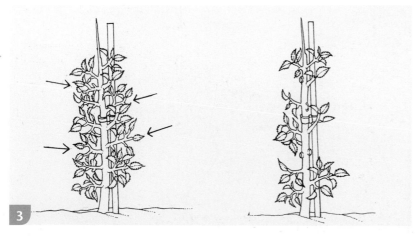

3 In late spring, some spur thinning can be done to prevent overcrowding; removing up to a third of the spurs from a spur system (*see* right) increases the size of the individual fruits. Remove any sucker growths or laterals forming below the head of the tree.

Plum 'Marjorie's Seedling'

Root pruning is a means of checking a tree's growth. It is most commonly carried out on fruit trees that are growing vigorously at the expense of cropping, but it is also a useful technique for restricting the growth of almost any tree that is in danger of growing too large for its position.

The reason root pruning is so often used to good effect with fruit trees is that the removal of some of the root system induces the formation of flower buds. Within a couple of years, fruit yields should improve. It works because the loss of roots puts the tree under stress and, like most plants under threat, it will attempt to reproduce itself before its demise.

From this it is obvious that root pruning should not be undertaken too often and, with large trees especially, it should be carried out over a two- or three-year period (pruning some of the roots one year, another section the next, and so on). However, once the tree has fully recovered and new strong roots begin to grow again (which will be evident from vigorous shoot growth), the desired effects of the root prune will dwindle and the operation may have be repeated.

Root pruning should be carried out only in winter when the tree is dormant. The best plan with trees less than five years old is to dig up the tree, cleanly cut away any large roots with a pruning saw or secateurs (leaving as much of the fine fibrous root as possible), and then replant. Care should be taken not to allow the fibrous roots to dry out before replanting in the same (or new, more desirable) position. Always replant the tree at the depth it was at originally.

With older trees, digging up and replanting is obviously not practical, so the operation must be carried out in situ by exposing a section of the root system 120–160cm from the trunk (see below). Old, mature trees should be treated in the same way, but the trench should be dug just outside the diameter of the tree's leaf canopy and the process spread over two or three winters.

After any root pruning operation, enrich the soil with well-rotted manure or garden compost and if necessary stake the tree to give it support (especially if it is in an exposed site).

If, after root pruning, a tree continues to put on too much growth, it is likely that the rootstock is of a variety that is too vigorous for the tree's situation; the only solution then is to replace the tree.

HOW TO root prune a tree

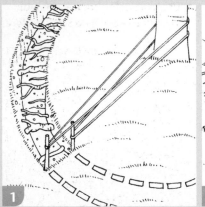

1 First measure out and then dig a trench around the tree. The inner edge of the trench should be 120–160cm (4–5ft) from the trunk, depending on the tree's age and size. As you dig, be careful not to damage the fine fibrous roots.

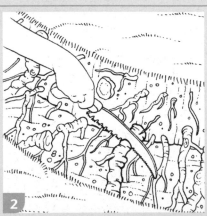

2 Having exposed this section of the root system, cut through and dispose of all the thick roots using a pruning saw or loppers. Once again, take great care not to damage the thin fibrous roots.

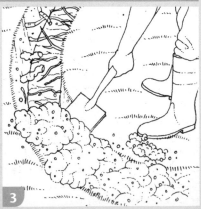

3 With the large roots removed, spread out the remaining fibrous roots in the trench. Refill the trench with the excavated soil, enriching it as you go with well-rotted manure or good garden compost. Firm the soil and water in well.

The self-fertile plum 'Purple Pershore' has a sharp flavour. It is one of the best culinary plums – perfect for jam.

Pruning columnar plums

Since these forms are supplied already pruned, most (if not all) of the formative pruning will already have been carried out. With the correct pruning, such a tree will continue to grow as a single column to about 2–2.5m (6–8ft) high, depending on the variety grown and the vigour of the rootstock on which it has been grafted.

Usually, after the formative pruning when the tree starts to crop regularly, little further pruning is required. A certain amount of pruning will be necessary during summer to make sure it keeps to the desired size and shape, to control the shoot growth and encourage the formation of fruit buds; some pruning in late spring may also be necessary. The aim is to grow a tree that has short fruit-bearing spurs over the branches on the column of growth, and prune in such a way as to encourage the tree to bear well-coloured, good-sized fruits.

Figs were traditionally grown fan-trained against a wall or other support – a good way of controlling their vigorous growth.

Figs

Figs are one of the oldest cultivated fruits and are believed to have been introduced to Britain by the Romans. They grow best in a warm, sunny position, with some protection from severe frost. In the right conditions, they can produce three crops of fruit each year, although only one of these flushes of fruit is likely to reach maturity. They were traditionally grown as a fan-trained tree against a wall or fence, and to control their vigorous growth and root spread they were usually planted into a flagstone-'lined' planting pit. Figs are now more commonly grown as a standard or half-standard tree in a container.

Training a standard fig tree

A standard must have a strong stem or 'leg' to support the framework of branches, or 'head'. Figs are naturally bushy plants and need to be trained to form a single straight stem before the bushy habit is allowed to prevail. They are propagated by cuttings or layering, so they grow on their own root system rather than on a rootstock.

Young figs (from a rooted cutting) usually have four to five stems close to ground level, and rather than try to straighten one of these stems it is better to make a new start and create a new main stem. The process of stem formation continues each year until the stem has reached approximately 30–45cm (12–18in) above the required stem height – usually a clear stem of 1.2m (4ft) is preferred.

The aim is then to develop a well-balanced head of shoots that radiate evenly from the central main stem. These are pruned to create a framework of multi-branched lateral shoots that allow plenty of light to reach all parts of the plant.

Figs are routinely pruned in spring, and in cooler climates may also need some pruning or pinching in summer. As well as encouraging the production of fruit-bearing stems, pruning should also be aimed at removing some of the older sections of branches and creating room for new, replacement shoots to develop.

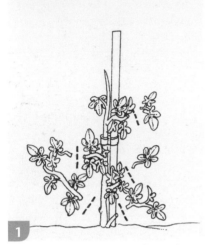

1

In the first spring, cut down all growth to 10–15cm (4–6in) above compost level. As new shoots grow, train the strongest up a cane, tying in at 25cm (10in) intervals. Remove the lower shoots and prune buds that start to develop to four leaves.

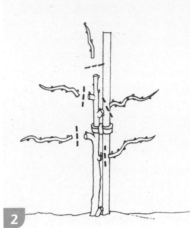

2

Next spring, remove any frost-damaged growth and prune back the lateral shoots to a single bud. Reduce the central leader by one third, cutting to a strong bud. Summer prune as before, and repeat in the third year if you want a longer clear stem.

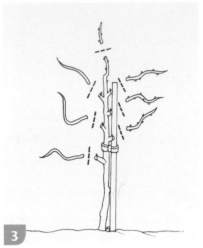

3

Next spring, remove the tip of the main stem, and cut back all the laterals to a single bud.

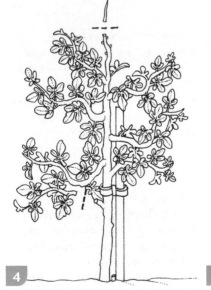

4

As the new shoots grow, select five or six and allow these to develop into a branch framework, evenly spaced around the main stem. If a new upright leader starts to form, cut it back to four buds.

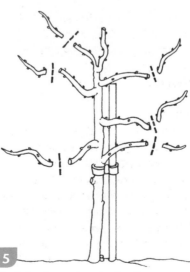

5

The following spring, shorten the framework branches to six buds. Remove any growth that might make a new central leader and any 'sucker' growths or laterals below the head of the tree.

Ficus carica 'Brunswick' – a vigorous and very hardy fig tree that bears good, fairly large fruits (reddish brown when mature). Its attractive, deeply lobed foliage makes it worth growing for its ornamental value, too.

1 In spring, remove any frost-damaged growth. Prune out inward-pointing shoots and buds to maintain an open centre. Cut back overlong and bare branches to 5cm (2in) to encourage new shoots to form.

2 In summer, shorten all the sideshoots from the main framework of branches back to five leaves, and pinch out any new shoots at five or six leaves to encourage fruit formation.

3 In early autumn, remove any fruit larger than small pea size as these will not develop. Leave the remaining tiny, embryo fruits to overwinter – usually they will ripen in the following year.

Stone fruits

Many of the 'stone' fruits such as almonds, apricots, cherries (sweet and acid), peaches and some varieties of plum will only grow well if they have some protection and shelter, especially in colder areas. In order to make this possible, gardeners resort to trained trees grown against a wall or fence to take advantage of the residual heat provided by the background support structure. The most

common and popular type of trained tree for these plants is the 'fan' (although this method of intensive production and pruning can reduce the life span of the plant).

The fan

This tree form is created by training a series of lateral shoots (ribs) and sublaterals, which radiate out in an arc from a short 'leg' or stem. These can be bought either as a part-trained fan-shaped tree or as a young tree with branches – a 'feathered maiden' – which can be planted and pruned to create the fan. This process normally takes three to four years.

In the early stages, formative pruning involves creating and training shoots of similar size which

spread out evenly to form a framework of shoots, or the 'ribs' of the fan. In order to achieve this shape, a structural support of horizontal wires and bamboo canes is needed to shape and hold the ribs in place. In the later stages, the focus of the pruning regime switches towards creating fruiting buds, with the ribs of the fan being allowed to extend and being tied into the support frame. Smaller branches growing from these ribs are the shoots that will carry the following year's blossom.

With routine pruning, the aim is to provide a constant supply of young shoots to replace the old cropping wood. This is usually done after harvesting the fruits. The

Don't forget

All stone fruits should be pruned in summer, wherever possible, to reduce the risk of infection from the fungus silver leaf or bacterial canker, which usually enter the tree through pruning wounds made in the winter.

A peach tree ('Peregrine') fan-trained against a brick wall, which gives it shelter and some residual warmth.

fruiting shoot is pruned out and replaced with a shoot from just below the point where the cut was made. This process must be carried out regularly to prevent the growth becoming congested and non-productive.

HOW TO fan-train a stone-fruit tree

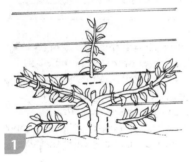

1

In the first year, remove all but the two framework branches that are trained to right and left as shown.

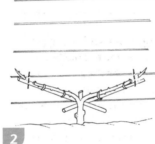

2

In the second winter, cut back the two side branches or 'ribs' to an upward-facing bud 45cm (18in) from the main stem.

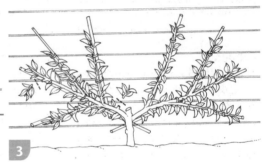

3

Through summer, tie in the new extension growth to the canes, and allow two or three suitably spaced shoots to grow on each branch. Tie these shoots to canes, and prune out any competing shoots as they grow, or cut them back to one bud.

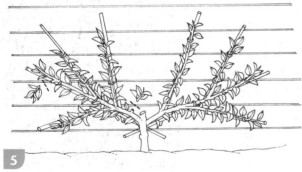

5

In summer, allow the leading shoots to grow and tie each into a cane. Keep two or three suitably spaced shoots to grow on each branch, and tie them to canes. Repeat this until a well branched fan fills the available space.

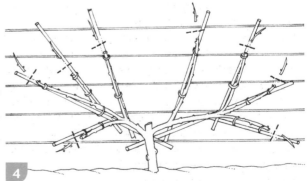

4

In the third spring, prune the end third of each shoot to leave mature wood from the previous season.

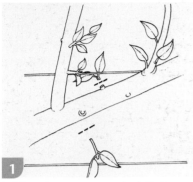

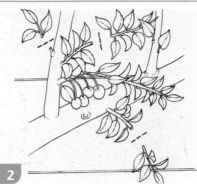

1 In late spring, remove any buds that are growing directly into the support structure or out at right angles from the fan structure and support.

2 In midsummer, select one or two replacements for each fruit-bearing shoot. Tie them to supports at about 10cm (4in) intervals and cut them back to six leaves.

3 In late summer, remove the shoots that fruited this year. Trim the selected replacement shoots back again to three leaves to encourage fruit buds to form.

Olives

The popularity of olive growing has increased greatly over recent years and, because self-fertile cultivars are now available, they can be grown as individual plants. Young plants are readily available for growing as a patio plant, or as a tree within a sheltered garden. They are slow-growing broad-leaved evergreens, widely grown in warmer climates, but they are quite hardy – most cultivars are capable of withstanding low temperatures (to freezing point). They actually need cool winters in order to crop well, although in more northerly locations they must have a sheltered spot to give them some winter protection.

Olive trees normally start to bear fruit four to five years after planting. Although they rarely reach more than 4m (13ft) tall in cooler areas, they do have a spreading habit and will develop a broad, spreading canopy unless they are pruned regularly.

With formative pruning, the aim is to develop a tree with clear leg or stem with a framework of four to five lateral branches radiating out from the stem above this point; these will form the main framework of branches. Because the plant keeps growing throughout the year, albeit more slowly in the winter, young shoot tips are often damaged by frost and will need to be pruned accordingly. During the early stages of development, the young trees need to be well staked to allow the main stem to form and thicken.

Young plants are often sold as part-trained standards, with some of the formative pruning already completed, or as bushes that need to be pruned to create the main stem or 'leg'. The process of stem formation continues each year until the tree is about 1.5m (5ft) high,

with a clear stem of 1–1.2m (3–4ft). The crown or 'head' of the tree often branches naturally, producing lots of dense, twiggy growth; pruning is therefore aimed at selecting the best-positioned shoots to form a well-balanced head of four

Olive trees are long-lived. Many will continue to produce fruit for well over a hundred years.

to five branches radiating out from the main stem, and stopping the central leader to control the overall height of the tree. It is important to create an open framework of branches to allow as much light as possible into the centre of the tree.

Routine pruning can be used to restrict the size of the tree, and to keep the head of the tree open so that sunlight can penetrate the centre. Fruits are borne on one-year-old stems, usually on the periphery of the tree canopy. Growth tends to be dense and bushy, so much of the pruning is aimed at thinning out congested shoots and removing old, unproductive wood to make room for younger replacement branches.

Prune to maintain a balance between new shoots and a regular crop of fruits. This is important because many olives have a tendency to slip into 'biennial bearing' – a heavy fruit crop one year followed by an extremely light crop the next. This can be minimized by pruning off a proportion of the fruiting wood after a light crop, or soon after fruit-set of a heavy crop.

Renovation

Olives respond well to hard pruning: they can be completely renovated by pruning to ground level.

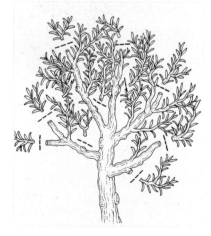

Routine pruning. In spring, remove old, unproductive wood in order to stimulate new flower-bearing shoots, and thin overcrowded shoots to keep an open centre. Prune back the branch leaders to promote new shoots and restrict the size of the tree.

HOW TO form a fruiting head on an olive tree

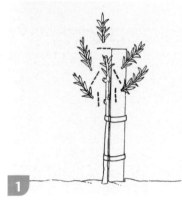

1

In spring, prune the central leader back to a strong bud about 1.5m (5ft) above ground level. Remove any 'sucker' growths emerging from lower down the main stem.

2

From the new growth, select four or five shoots within the top 30cm (1ft) of the stem to form branches, plus one to replace the central leader. Remove any other competing shoots.

3

In late summer, prune the replacement leader back to a single bud. Allow the dense, twiggy crown to develop with minimal pruning.

4

The following spring, prune out any frost damage and shorten lateral shoots to 30cm (12in) to encourage branching. Remove any shoots on the central leader.

Citrus plants

These plants need plenty of sunlight to grow well, and often lose many of their leaves in the winter when the light levels are poor. The young stems are green and often function like leaves. Initial pruning is aimed at getting a bushy plant with balanced growth and a well-developed framework of branches. After this, no major pruning is required, although the stems are often bare after winter leaf-fall, so branches and shoots can be shortened by up to two thirds every other year.

The best time to prune a citrus plant is in early spring, but care needs to be taken as the plant will often have flowers and fruits on the shoots at the same time; pruning is therefore often continuous throughout the year.

An orange tree – growing in a wooden planter in a Mediterranean-style garden – bears good-sized fruits in midsummer.

Don't forget

Severe pruning can kill citrus plants, as they store very little food in the woody tissue.

HOW TO train a citrus bush tree

1

In spring, prune the stem of the young plant by about a third, cutting above a leaf.

2

In summer, when new laterals shoot from the pruned main stem, prune them back to half their length. (Any weak ones should be pruned back harder to encourage bushiness.) Pinch out any shoots that appear on the stem (do not pinch out stem leaves).

3

In spring, prune the branch leaders by a third. Prune the tips of any strong leaders and cut back crossing shoots to an outward-facing bud. Continue in this way until an open but well-balanced crown has been achieved.

A–Z pruning directory

It's vital to understand the general principles and techniques of pruning, as described earlier, but because individual plants have particular requirements you should also familiarize yourself with the specific needs of all the plants in your garden. It's no good hazarding a guess as to how to prune – obvious as it may seem, once a branch has been removed, there's no putting it back! On the following pages you'll find a quick, plant-by-plant reference guide to ensure you use the right pruning method at the right time. (For fruit pruning, *see* pages 94–123.)

KEY: DT = deciduous tree, DS = deciduous shrub, DCL = deciduous climber, ECL = evergreen climber, ES = evergreen shrub/sub-shrub, ET = evergreen tree, HCL = herbaceous climber, SES = semi-evergreen shrub

Plant name	When to prune	How to prune
Abeliophyllum distichum (white forsythia) DS	Spring, after flowering	Train against a wall for a neater habit: tie in strong shoots and cut one third or half of the sideshoots to low buds. In later years, clear out any sparse stems. Prune freestanding plants as for *Forsythia*.
Abies (silver fir) ET	Spring	Little pruning or training is needed, but cut out any shoots that compete with the main leading shoot.
Abutilon ES/DS	Late winter–early spring	Cut back deciduous shoots by up to a half to tidy away old flowered shoots or to the main framework to produce larger leaves; prune evergreen types lightly to preserve their natural shapes.
Acacia (mimosa, wattle) Evergreen types	After flowering	Lightly trim to tidy flowered shoots; don't cut into old wood.
Deciduous types	Late winter–early spring	Cut out crossing or misshapen shoots to keep a good shape.
Acer (maple) DT/DS	Late autumn–midwinter	After formative shaping, regular pruning is unnecessary and best avoided, since maples bleed readily. Just remove dead shoot tips or misplaced stems when the plant is dormant.
Actinidia kolomikta DCL	Late winter–early spring, before growth begins	Keep plant within its allotted space by shortening long stems by one third to a half. Also, remove an entire old stem from time to time, to spur new growth from the base.
Alnus (alder) DT	Autumn–midwinter, after leaf fall	Mature trees don't need much pruning, apart from removing awkwardly placed branches. Alders bleed when pruned.
Amelanchier (snowy mespilus) DS	Winter	Regular pruning is unnecessary, but shoots on multi-stemmed plants can twist around each other if not thinned out. *A. stolonifera* has a suckering habit: remove shoots at the base.
Ampelopsis DCL	Late winter–spring	Little pruning is needed, except for cutting back rampant stems to keep them clear of the gutters and roof.
Aralia elata DS	Early spring, before growth starts	Avoid regular pruning, but trim off frost-damaged tips, remove suckers and, on variegated plants, reverted green shoots.
Arbutus ET	Spring, when risk of frost is past	No pruning necessary, except to keep it healthy: small branches may die off within the canopy and should be cut out at the base; also remove branches that are clogging the centre.
Argyranthemum ES	Throughout the growing season	Respond well to pinch pruning, so can be used to create topiary. With finger and thumb, remove the shoot tips to make them bushy. Stop pruning a month or two before you want the plant to flower.
Aristolochia macrophylla (Dutchman's pipe) DCL	Late winter–early spring	Cut out any weak growth and keep fast-growing shoots from outgrowing their space by cutting them back to within 2–3 buds from the main stems.
Artemisia abrotanum, A. arborescens, A. ludoviciana DS	Spring, just after the buds burst	Prune the woody base to 15–30cm (6–12in) and leave 1–2 buds on each stem. Don't neglect maintenance pruning – they don't respond well to renovation. Artemisias are suitable for topiary.
Aucuba japonica ES (spotted laurel)	Mid-spring, after winter show of berries, and summer	In the first year, remove spindly shoots and cut back strong stems by one third; later, in summer, take out crossing shoots and flower buds. Thereafter, cut out flowered and spindly shoots in spring and trim over-strong shoots by one third in summer. Phase renovation by cutting one third of the stems to the ground.
Azara microphylla ET/ES	Late spring	Train this tender plant against a wall for extra protection. Cut back wayward stems to the allotted space, hard prune weak shoots to stimulate stronger growth, and tie in new stems.
Banksia ET/ES	After flowering	Trim old stems lightly to restrict the size. *B. integrifolia* and *B. menziesii* tolerate hard pruning, but *B. coccinea* and *B. spinulosa* do not.

Plant name	When to prune	How to prune
Berberis (barberry) Evergreen types	In early summer, after flowering, or autumn–winter after fruiting	Cut out only thin and flowered shoots; trim excessively arching stems by one third in summer. It will stand drastic reduction to 30cm (12in) from the base. Suitable for topiary or an informal hedge.
Deciduous types	Late winter–early spring	Take one fifth of the stems out at the base, or to a strong, low shoot, each year to keep the plant looking vigorous. It makes a good formal or informal hedge – trim with secateurs.
B. × *ottawensis* DS	Late winter–early spring	For the showiest foliage, coppice cultivars of this species. In the first year, cut all stems by one third and remove weak shoots. The second year, cut all stems to 5–8cm (2–3in) above soil level. Repeat every other year.
Betula (birch) DT	Late summer–midwinter, when fully dormant	Best pruned as little as possible, since they bleed copiously. Remove competing leaders from young trees and any twiggy growth on trunks. Clear dead stems from below the canopies of weeping forms.
Bougainvillea ECL/DCL	Late winter–early spring	Tidy up the shape by cutting out a few older or crowded stems at the base and cut wandering shoots to keep them within the outline. For a fine show of blooms, spur prune the sideshoots back to 2–3 buds.
Brachyglottis (senecio) ES	Summer, after flowering	Lightly clip to remove flowered shoots and shorten leggy top-growth.
	Mid-spring, after risk of frost is past	Straggly plants respond well to phased renovation – chop down half or two thirds of the stems each year for 2–3 years.
Brugmansia (angel's trumpet) ET/ES	Late winter, before growth begins	Give the plant a good haircut, reducing all last year's stems to 15cm (6in) of the main stems or the base, to stimulate new flowering shoots and keep the plant a manageable size. It reacts well to hard renewal pruning, if needed.
Buddleja (butterfly bush), most species DS	Midsummer, after flowering	Cut out flowered stems to a healthy bud or shoot, to keep a balanced shape. Prune standards similarly to create a well-shaped head and renew flowering shoots.
B. davidii DS	Spring	Needs regular hard pruning. In the first spring, shorten all main stems by two thirds and cut sideshoots to 2–3 buds. In the second spring, reduce the new growth by half, cut out all weak stems and one third of crowded shoots. In following years, reduce main stems by one third, sideshoots to 2–3 buds and remove old, exhausted shoots.
	Mid-autumn	Cut back tall stems, if needed, to protect the shrub from wind rock.
B. globosa DS	Late winter, before growth begins	Remove any dead or weak shoots. If you don't mind losing this year's flower buds, cut long stems back by up to one third. You can also chop tip-flowering stems back to old wood to spur new, vigorous growth.
Buxus (box) ET/ES	Late spring	Trim off frost damage, shear hedges, or cut shrubs hard down to 15–30cm (6–12in) if they need renovation.
	Late summer–early winter	In early years, trim sideshoots for bushy growth. Cut out reverted shoots from variegated plants. Give hedges or topiary a second trim.
Callicarpa bodinieri var. *giraldii* (beauty berry) DS	Winter (for berries)	Thin out every year to avoid overcrowding: cut out one fifth of the old, distorted stems at the base. You may be able to resurrect a frost-damaged plant by lopping off all dead stems at the base.
Callistemon (bottlebrush) DS	Summer, after flowering	Regular pruning is unnecessary, but you can shorten leggy top-growth to young shoots.
	Late winter or early spring	This plant responds well to phased renovation, if necessary – cut half or two thirds of the stems back hard over 2–3 years.
Calluna vulgaris (heather) ES	Mid- or late spring	As growth begins, prune out weak basal shoots to spur new stems.
	Early summer, after flowering	Shear off spent shoots.

Plant name	When to prune	How to prune
Calycanthus DS	Spring	Usually needs little pruning, but it produces new shoots from the base and may be pruned back hard, leaving only the youngest stems.
Camellia C. chrysantha, C. lutchuensis, C. sasanqua ES	Late summer–early winter	After planting, remove tips of competing leaders; in early years, trim sideshoots to form a bushy plant; thereafter, little pruning is needed.
	Spring, before buds break	Trim off any frosted tips. Renovate as for *C. japonica*.
	Early summer, after flowering	Dead-head to remove tatty, faded blooms. Take care not to damage the new shoots below the flowers.
C. hiemalis, C. japonica, C. reticulata, C. × williamsii ES	Mid-spring	In first 3 years, remove weak and crossing branches to create an open framework. Then, each year, remove weak shoots, cut back by one third any over-long stems, and cut the last season's growth to just above the old wood to create a dense, free-flowering bush. Phase renovation over 3 years, if necessary.
	Early summer, after flowering	Dead-head regularly (*see C. chrysantha*).
Campsis (trumpet vine) DCL	Late winter–early spring	It takes 2–3 years of cutting shoots down to 15cm (6in) to establish a strong framework. Then you need simply to spur prune all sideshoots to 2–3 buds. Cut any damaged main stems to the base.
Caragana DT/DS	Late winter–early spring	Light pruning required – shortening long, spent flowering stems helps young plants to bush out into elegant shapes, but after that most need little attention. You can train *C. arborescens* as a standard.
Carpenteria californica ES	Spring	Cut out no more than one third of older stems at the base occasionally.
Carpinus betulus (hornbeam) DT/DS	After flowering	Lightly trim flowered shoots and any wispy stems.
	Late winter–early spring	If needed, renovate a hedge by cutting back hard one side of the hedge, then do the same on the other side in the following year.
	Spring	Coppice for a multi-stemmed shrub or hedging – cut all stems down to 15cm (6in), then retain 4–5 of the new shoots. Shear formal hedges in late spring.
Caryopteris × *clandonensis*	Late summer–early autumn	Give hedges a second trim (lightly on young hedges).
	Spring	In the first year, shorten all main stems by two thirds and cut sideshoots to 2–3 buds. In the second year, reduce the new growth by half, cut out all weak stems and one third of crowded shoots. Thereafter, reduce main stems by one third, laterals to 2–3 buds and completely remove old, unproductive shoots.
Catalpa bignonioides (Indian bean tree) DT	Autumn–late winter	Little pruning is needed for a tree, but you can pollard it to remedy damage or get even bigger leaves. Prune all stems back to the main branches about 1.2m (4ft) above ground level.
Ceanothus (California lilac) Evergreen types	Early spring	Lightly prune last year's growth. Prune the same growth by one third to half on wall-trained shrubs and remove shoots growing in the wrong direction. Don't cut into old wood.
	Late summer	Shorten all new sideshoots to 2–3 leaves for more flower buds next year and to show off the berries. Avoid removing stems with developing buds.
Deciduous types	Late winter or early spring	Phased renovation over 2–3 years works well – cut half or two thirds of the stems back hard, if necessary.
	Spring	Reduce main stems by one third, laterals to 2–3 buds and completely remove old, unproductive shoots.
Celastrus orbiculatus (bittersweet) DCL	Winter–early spring	Too much pruning favours leafy shoots over flowers and fruits, so leave scrambling plants alone, apart from digging out suckers. On trained climbers, cut out badly placed stems and cut back long shoots.

Plant name	When to prune	How to prune
Ceratostigma willmottianum (plumbago) DS	Spring, just after the buds burst	Plumbago often dies back in cold areas, almost to the ground. Prune the woody base to within 15–30cm (6–12in) and each stem to 1–2 buds. If not affected, cut out old, flowered shoots.
Cercidiphyllum japonicum (Katsura tree) DT	Autumn–late winter, when dormant	Trees may be single- or multi-stemmed and are best left to follow their natural form. Little pruning needed, but remove frost damage.
Cercis (Judas tree) DT/DS	Early summer (to avoid infection from coral spot)	Prune only to remove damaged or crossing shoots. Pollard to renovate listing trees or make the most of showy foliage – in dry weather, cut down almost to ground level and select 4–5 of the strongest shoots for the new framework.
Cestrum ES/DS	Late winter–early spring	Tip prune young plants for bushiness. Thin 2- or 3-year-old stems, cutting at the base. If cold has killed off the top-growth, cut hard back in early spring to prompt the plant to regenerate.
Chaenomeles (Japanese quince) DS	Late spring	Cut back excess growth. Prune hard to renovate, if necessary.
	Midsummer	Reduce sideshoots to 3–5 leaves, or clip a *C. speciosa* hedge, for more flowering spurs. Cut back shoots to main stems of wall-trained plants.
Chamaecyparis lawsoniana (Lawson cypress) ET	Late spring–autumn	Trim this conifer regularly to keep it neat, if grown as a hedge, or reduce untidy sideshoots on trees, but don't cut into old wood.
Chamaerops humilis (dwarf fan palm)	When necessary	No regular pruning needed, but cut off dead or damaged leaves towards the base. Don't cut into the trunk; leave a neat stub.
Chimonanthus praecox (wintersweet) DS	Late winter, after flowering	Doesn't need regular pruning, but responds to renewal pruning. Training on a sunny wall helps it to survive cold winters – reduce flowered shoots to 2–3 buds and cut out old or weak stems.
Choisya ternata (Mexican orange blossom) ES	Spring, after flowering	These are naturally well shaped, so need little attention, although cutting off flowered shoots above a healthy bud may reward you with a second flush. Rejuvenate old shrubs by hard pruning.
Chrysanthemum	Throughout the growing season	Respond well to pinch pruning, so you can get creative and produce your own containerized topiary.
Cistus (rock rose) ES	Spring	Tip prune young plants to help them bush out. Mature plants don't like being pruned, so just trim off frost damage. Old, sparse plants are best replaced.
Citrus (ornamental citrus) ET/ES	Late winter–early spring	Prune lightly, taking out wayward shoots. Grafted lemon cultivars need severe pruning to remove water shoots and suckers, and to maintain a compact crown.
Clematis (*see* pages 79–81 for definitions of pruning groups) Group 1 (early-flowering) ECL/DCL	Spring, after flowering	Shear off spent flowering shoots, shorten over-long stems and cut back up to one third of the oldest stems on evergreen clematis.
Group 2 (twice-flowering) DCL	Late winter–early spring, as buds burst	Remove weak growth and reduce stems by one third to healthy buds, preferably about 1m (40in) above soil level. Tie in new shoots.
	Midsummer	Trim immediately after the first flush to encourage later flowering.
Group 3 (late-flowering) DCL	Late winter–early spring, as buds burst	Cut down to about 30cm (12in), to strong buds on each stem, then reduce weak shoots to buds at the base. Tie in new shoots.
Clerodendrum C. bungei (glory flower) DS	Spring, when buds begin to break	The first year, shorten all main stems by two thirds and cut sideshoots to 2–3 buds. In the second year, reduce the new growth by half, cut out all weak stems and one third of crowded shoots. Thereafter, reduce main stems by one third, sideshoots to 2–3 buds and remove old, unproductive shoots or frost-damaged shoots.
C. trichotomum DS	Late winter–early spring	The first year, cut stems by one third and remove weak shoots. The second year, coppice by cutting all stems to 5–8cm (2–3in) above soil level and repeat every year. Dig out and tear off suckers.

Plant name	When to prune	How to prune
Clethra C. *alnifolia* (sweet pepper bush) DS	Late winter–early spring	Regular pruning is unnecessary. Treat like *Amelanchier stolonifera*.
C. *arborea* (lily-of-the-valley tree) ES	Late winter–early spring	Leave unpruned, except to take out older branches to make way for younger growth.
Colletia hystrix DS	Late winter–early spring	The first year, cut stems by one third and remove weak shoots. The second year, coppice for colourful stems and thorns by cutting all stems to 5–8cm (2–3in) above soil level and repeat every year.
Colutea (bladder senna) DS	Spring	Needs little pruning, apart from cutting back wayward shoots. If cut back hard, like *Cornus alba*, you can keep it small.
Convolvulus cneorum ES	Mid-spring	Cut out any damaged shoots.
	Late summer, after flowering	Trim spent and wayward shoots to shape.
Cordyline australis ET	Any time	No pruning needed, but cut off damaged/dead leaves at the base.
Cornus (dogwood), most species DS	Early spring	Regular pruning is unnecessary, except to keep its shape or spread. Remove up to one quarter of the oldest stems to keep it in check.
C. *alba*, C. *sanguinea* DS	Early spring	Grown mainly for their colourful stems: in the first year, cut stems back by one third and remove weak shoots. The second year, coppice for the brightest bark – cut all stems to 5–8cm (2–3in) above soil level and repeat every year.
C. *sericea* (red osier dogwood) DS	Early spring	As for C. *alba*, but prune in alternate years, or cut only two thirds of the stems each year.
Coronilla ES/DS	Early spring	Don't prune, except to cut out old, exhausted stems at the base. These shrubs don't recover well from hard pruning into old wood.
Corylopsis DS	Early to mid-spring, after flowering	Regular pruning is unnecessary and would spoil the natural elegance of the shrub. Just remove any branches that interfere with its shape.
Corylus (hazel), most species DS	Early spring	Cut out wayward shoots or suckers. Coppice for multi-stemmed hedging – cut all stems to 15cm (6in), then allow 4–5 of the new shoots to develop.
C. *avellana*, C. *maxima* DS	Late winter–early spring	In the first year, cut stem(s) by one third and remove weak shoots. The second year, coppice to get large leaves by cutting all stems to 5–8cm (2–3in) above soil level and repeat every year.
C. *avellana* 'Contorta' DS	Winter	Once this slow-grower reaches a decent size, take out entire branches to keep it neat, reduce the weight of sideshoots, and to encourage fresh, twisty stems. Remove suckers at the base.
Cotinus coggygria (smoke bush) DS	Spring, before growth begins	Leave unpruned for a prolific flowering display. If you want the best foliage, for example from C. *coggygria* 'Royal Purple', in the first year, cut the stems by one third and remove weak shoots. In subsequent years, coppice by cutting all stems to 5–8cm (2–3in) above soil level.
Cotoneaster Deciduous types	Mid-spring	Most need little or no pruning, apart from taking out unhealthy or spindly growth. Prune wall-trained shrubs, cutting out unproductive stems and prune to shape if needed. Can be hard pruned.
	Late summer, after flowering	On wall shrubs, shorten all new sideshoots to 2–3 leaves for more flower buds next year and to expose this year's berries. Retain stems with developing buds. Cut back long shoots on informal hedges and trim new shoots to the berry clusters after flowering.
Evergreen types	Late summer, after flowering	Lightly trim dwarf evergreens to shape.
C. × *watereri* DS	Late winter–early spring (for berries)	Cut all stems to 2–3 buds of the framework.

Plant name	When to prune	How to prune
Crataegus monogyna (hawthorn) DS	Early summer–late winter	Shear hedges after the flowers fade. Renovate by cutting down to the base. Shrubs are naturally congested; remove only rubbing stems.
Cryptomeria japonica (Japanese cedar) ET	Spring	This conifer needs little pruning. Rejuvenate untidy plants by cutting all stems to 60–90cm (2–3ft).
× *Cupressocyparis leylandii* (Leyland cypress) ET	Late spring	Prune formal hedges every year without cutting into old wood.
	Late summer–early autumn	Give it a second trim to restrict size.
Cupressus (cypress) ET	Spring	No regular pruning is needed, except to remove shoots that compete with the leader. If growing *C. macrocarpa* (Monterey cypress) as a hedge or for topiary, trim without cutting into old wood.
Cytisus (broom), most species DS	Summer, after flowering	Tip prune young plants. Cut back flowered shoots on mature plants to 2–3 buds above the main stems, but don't cut into old wood.
C. battandieri (pineapple broom) SES	Summer, after flowering	Needs little pruning, but on wall-trained plants cut out an old stem from time to time to renew the framework; tie in the new shoot later.
Daboecia cantabrica (heath) ES	Mid-spring–early summer	Prune out weak shoots at the base to encourage new growth.
	After flowering	Shear off spent shoots.
Daphne DS	Late winter–early spring	Prune only if really necessary – it could cause dieback.
Davidia involucrata (dove tree, ghost tree, handkerchief tree) DT	Late winter–early spring	Little pruning is needed, apart from taking out shoots that compete with the central leader in early years. Later, simply keep a balanced shape by removing any awkwardly placed branches.
Decaisnea fargesii DS	Late winter–early spring	Just cut out any shoot that may spoil the shape.
Deutzia DS	Summer, after flowering	Cut one fifth of the oldest stems to 5–8cm (2–3in) above soil level to keep a good supply of new, strong shoots from the base. Remove frost-damaged and spent flowered shoots, down to a healthy bud.
Diervilla	Early spring, as buds break	Cut back the entire plant hard each year to about 30cm (12in). Old plants are best divided rather than renewal pruned.
Dipelta floribunda DS	Midsummer, after flowering	Cut one fifth of the oldest stems to the base, especially any that show signs of dieback, to stimulate new, young shoots, and cut back remaining flowered shoots to strong buds.
Eccremocarpus scaber (Chilean glory flower) ECL	Spring	Cut out frost-damaged shoots. If the plant has died back to the ground, wait for the new shoots to appear and trim each to a strong bud to encourage them to throw up dense, bushy growth. These tender plants are better replaced than renovated.
Elaeagnus ES/DS	Late winter–early spring (deciduous) and mid- to late spring (evergreens)	Cut back straggly and overgrown stems, or any that spoil the shape, and reverted green stems from variegated plants. Trim formal hedges using secateurs.
Elsholtzia stauntonii (mint shrub) DS	Late winter	Cut back last year's flowering shoots hard and clear out twiggy or weak stems.
Embothrium coccineum (Chilean fire bush) ET/ES	Late winter–early spring	Cut out any straggly or wayward stems; remove suckers at the base.
Erica (low-growing heaths) ES	Mid- or late spring to early summer	As growth begins, prune out weak shoots at the base to encourage new growth, then, after flowering, shear off spent shoots.
E. arborea (tree heath) ES	Late spring–early summer	Once established, just prune to keep plants bushy and compact. Cut back shoots to 3–4 buds at the base or on a main stem.
Escallonia ES	Spring	Neglected plants tolerate hard pruning.
	Late summer, after flowering	Little regular pruning is required on freestanding shrubs. Cut out spent flowering stems on wall-trained shrubs to new sideshoots. Trim hedges to shape/cut back long stems to within the body of the hedge.

Plant name	When to prune	How to prune
Eucalyptus (gum tree) Evergreen types	Spring	Trees need no pruning, but coppice *E. gunnii* to keep the juvenile, rounded leaves and a short, bushy plant – use a saw to cut all stems to 15cm (6in), then allow one or 4–5 shoots to grow. If you want the patterned bark, you have to let the plant grow into a large tree.
Deciduous types	Late winter–spring	In the first year, cut stem(s) by one third and remove weak shoots. The second year, coppice to create smaller, multi-stemmed shrubs by cutting all stems to 5–8cm (2–3in) above soil level. Repeat every year.
Eucryphia ET	Late winter–spring	Tip prune young plants and cut out distorted or damaged branches, but don't over-prune if you want a good show of flowers.
Euonymus (spindle tree) Evergreen types	Mid-spring–late spring	Lightly trim to encourage bushiness, or to maintain the shape of a hedge. Cut out reverted green shoots on variegated plants. On wall-trained plants, cut out old, tired stems completely; tie in as they grow.
Deciduous types	Late winter–early spring	No need for regular pruning; just cut out a few stems at the base if needed to open up a crowded centre.
Euphorbia characias, *E. myrsinites, E. pulcherrima* (milkweed, spurge) ES	Midsummer, after flowering	Cut back flowered shoots to the base or a low, new sideshoot, taking care not to damage the new stems. Renovate a plant by chopping it to the ground; you'll lose a season's flowers but gain a sturdier shrub.
Exochorda (pearl bush) DS	Late spring, after flowering	Cut back flowered shoots to healthy buds or shoots and remove weak or crowded growth. To renovate an old, tired shrub, prune up to one third of old stems at the base.
Fagus sylvatica (beech) DT	Late winter–early spring and late summer–early autumn	The tree normally needs no attention but hedges do. For multi-stemmed hedging, coppice each plant by cutting all stems to 15cm (6in), then allow 4–5 of the new shoots to form the framework. Trim a formal hedge with secateurs. Renovate a hedge by cutting back hard one side only, then the other side the following year. Give hedges a second trim in late summer or early autumn.
Fallopia baldschuanica (Russian vine, mile-a-minute plant) DCL	Early spring	The main function of pruning is to keep it within bounds and remove suckers. Beware – unless you have a huge garden, this plant can easily become a monster.
× *Fatshedera* ES	Late summer	Cut back wayward shoots to within the outline of wall-trained plants.
Fatsia japonica (false castor oil plant) ES	Mid-spring	Normally, this slow-growing, large shrub needs little attention. Cut out sparse or long stems at the base. Can be trained as a wall shrub.
Ficus benjamina (weeping fig) ET/ES	Late summer–early autumn (to avoid bleeding)	Remove awkwardly placed or over-long stems.
Forsythia DS	Late spring, after flowering	Cut one fifth of oldest stems to 5–8cm (2–3in) above soil level to keep established shrubs looking jaunty, and cut down each flowered shoot to just above a young sideshoot that hasn't flowered.
Fothergilla DS	Late winter–early spring	Regular pruning is unnecessary, apart from cutting out crossing or twiggy shoots.
Fremontodendron ES	Midsummer, after flowering	Freestanding shrubs get by without much attention. Wall shrubs are easy too: shorten outward-growing stems and spent flowering shoots. Hard pruning doesn't give good results.
Fuchsia hybrids ES/DS	Spring–autumn	Finger prune sideshoots to shape and produce your own containerized topiary, as for *Argyranthemum*.
	Midsummer	Now is the time to train a fuchsia as a standard (*see* page 60).
F. magellanica (hardy fuchsia) DS	Early spring, just after bud burst	Cut down the woody base to 15–30 cm (6–12in) and 1–2 buds on each stem. For an infomal hedge that has survived the frosts, cut the sideshoots to low, healthy buds. Renovate a gappy hedge by cutting alternate plants to the base over 2 years.

Plant name	When to prune	How to prune
Garrya elliptica (silk-tassel bush) ES	Mid-spring	Remove thin shoots and cut back by one-third any over-long stems. You can also train it as a wall shrub or plant it as an informal hedge. Hack a plant right back to renovate it or keep it from spreading.
Genista (broom) DS	Late winter–early spring	Nip out young shoots to make them bushier, and keep plant lightly trimmed, taking out any unhealthy or spindly growth; don't cut into old wood, since it won't regrow. Tired shrubs are best replaced.
Ginkgo biloba (maidenhair tree) DT	Late winter–early spring	Prune as little as possible, just removing any misshapen or crossing branches. Cut shoots may die back.
Gleditsia triacanthos (honey locust) DT	Late summer–midwinter	Little pruning is required; remove unhealthy growth and any suckers.
Grevillea ES	Mid-spring	Cut out frost-damaged shoots. On feathered trees, cut out competing leaders, crossing branches and regrowth at the base. On wall-trained plants, shorten sub-laterals to 1–2 buds.
Griselinia littoralis ES	Mid-late spring	Prune lightly to preserve the rounded shape; cut out any frost-damaged growth. Plants will grow back strongly if pruned hard.
	Early–midsummer	Trim formal hedge with secateurs.
Gynura aurantiaca (velvet plant) ES	Mid-spring	Cut all stems down to 8cm (3in) and pinch out growing tips to stop this sub-shrub from getting leggy.
Halesia (silver bell, snowdrop tree) DT/DS	Autumn–early spring	Little pruning is needed. Remove some older wood if flowering is poor. You can train a young, multi-stemmed plant into a tree by cutting out all but the strongest stem.
Hamamelis (witch hazel) DS	Early spring, before leaves unfurl	Regular pruning is unnecessary and these slow-growing shrubs respond slowly; remove suckers if necessary.
Hebe (veronica) ES	Spring, after flowering	Clip with shears to shorten leggy or frost-damaged top-growth, pruning hard to stimulate fresh, new shoots. Trim again to remove spent flowering shoots and keep a tidy shape.
Hedera (ivy) ECL	Early spring, before growth begins	Prune to contain the plant, particularly from spreading into gutters, roofs and over fences. Hard pruning will result in vigorous regrowth.
Helianthemum (rock rose) ES	Midsummer–late summer, after flowering	Cut back stems lightly to encourage flowering and keep the plant neat. Left unpruned, these plants build up a tangle of old stems.
Helichrysum ES	Spring	Cut out frost damage and reduce leggy stems; regularly pinch out growing tips to make a bushy plant.
Hibiscus H. rosa-sinensis ES	Late spring	Cut back main stems by one third and sideshoots to 2–3 buds. Completely remove dead wood, to avoid coral spot.
H. syriacus DS	Late spring	Regular pruning is unnecessary, but cut any stems with dieback to live wood. If plants become unbalanced, cut back hard any sprawling branches and lightly prune upright stems.
Hippophae DS	Summer	Little pruning is needed. Cut out crowded shoots and outlying suckers at the base, but don't prune hard or more suckers will spring up.
Hoheria	Late spring	Cut back any frost-damaged growth to a healthy bud. Shorten any over-long or crowded stems on wall-trained forms.
	Summer, after flowering	Prune young plants as standards.
Humulus lupulus (hop) DCL	Early spring	Chop off the dead stems at ground level.
Hydrangea H. anomala subsp. *petiolaris* (climbing hydrangea) DCL	Summer, after flowering	Prune to keep the climber within bounds: thin out crowded shoots to the main stems, cut back long stems and reduce weak stems to 2–3 buds. Renovation pruning will work, if necessary.

Plant name	When to prune	How to prune
Hydrangea arborescens, *H. paniculata*	Mid-spring	In the second spring, reduce the new growth by half, cut out all weak stems and one third of crowded shoots. In later years, reduce main stems by one third, sideshoots to 2–3 buds and remove old, unproductive shoots.
H. macrophylla, H. serrata	Mid-spring	Dead-head, taking care not to damage new shoots below the flowers.
Hypericum calycinum (rose of Sharon) ES	Mid-spring	Needs little or no pruning, apart from taking out any unhealthy or spindly growth.
Idesia polycarpa DT	Late winter, when dormant	Lightly shape by removing crossing or wayward stems (hard pruning results in whippy water shoots). Makes a good standard.
Ilex (holly) Evergreen trees	After planting	Remove tips of competing leaders.
	Summer–early winter	Trim sideshoots of young plants for bushy growth; hard prune mature plants if necessary.
	Spring	Pruning is minimal; cut out frost-damaged stems and remove reverted shoots from variegated cultivars.
Evergreen shrubs	Mid-spring	Cut out weak stems and cut the remainder to just above soil level. Heavy pruning of neglected shrubs produces a good batch of vigorous new stems.
Indigofera DS	Early–mid-spring	Cut out weak stems.
Jacaranda ET	Winter, when dormant	To enjoy the ferny foliage on a container plant, train it as a feathered tree: cut out crossing or strongly vertical sideshoots and competing leaders and regrowth on the lower stem.
Jasminum nudiflorum (winter jasmine) DS	Mid-spring	Extremely tough but floppy, this looks better trained through evergreen shrubs, ivy or on trellis, and is perfect for north-facing walls. Shear off the dead flowerheads and the shoot tips of trained plants. If growing it more informally, take out the flowered shoots where they join the main stems. Renew old jasmines by completely removing a few old stems each year for several years.
Juglans (walnut) DT	Late summer (to avoid bleeding)	Keep pruning to a minimum – walnuts bleed copiously and don't take kindly to hard pruning.
Juniperus ET/ES	Late spring	Most junipers manage happily without pruning. Cut back a few stems of prostrate forms to contain the spread.
Kalmia ES	Late winter–spring	Stage renovation of leggy shrubs over a few years; *K. angustifolia* will bounce back after being totally chopped in one year.
	Summer, after flowering	Dead-head flower clusters to avoid masses of seeds.
Kerria japonica DS	Late winter–early spring	Coppice by cutting all canes to 5–8cm (2–3in) above soil level. Vary the height of the cuts to get flowers at different levels. Chop outlying suckers free with a spade.
Koelreuteria DT	Winter, when dormant	Do no more than cut out unhealthy growth.
Kolkwitzia amabilis (beauty bush) DS	Midsummer, after flowering	Thin about one third of the oldest, suckering shoots, cutting to a low sideshoot or the base to encourage fresh new shoots. Cut completely to ground level to renovate.
Laburnum (golden rain) DT	Late summer	Specimen trees don't need pruning, but the flowers look lovely hanging from trained plants. Trim all sideshoots to 2–4 buds.
Lagerstroemia ET/ES/DT/DS	Autumn–early spring	In frost-prone areas, train on walls or as multi-stemmed trees for maximum flowering sideshoots and sub-laterals. Cut back one third of these to the main stems, and thin if the centre is crowded.
Lantana ES	Late winter	Train standards for the conservatory by pinch pruning, as for *Fuchsia* hybrids.

Plant name	When to prune	How to prune
Lathyrus latifolius (perennial pea) HCL	Autumn, after flowering or early spring, before growth begins	Pinch prune young plants to make them bushier. In cooler regions, this woody based perennial dies back in winter: remove all dead growth to the base. In warmer areas, cut out any unhealthy or spindly shoots after flowering.
Laurus nobilis (sweet bay, bay laurel) ET	Spring, before growth begins	Prune overcrowded border shrubs severely, cutting into old wood.
	Summer	Clip or tip prune hedges, standards and topiary.
Lavandula (lavender) ES	Mid-spring–late spring	Shorten leggy top-growth to keep the plant compact.
	Late summer, after flowering	Shear over plants and shape hedges, trimming to low buds just beyond the base of the old flower stems. Don't prune into old wood.
Lavatera (mallow) DS	Spring	In the second year, reduce the new growth by half, cut out all weak and one third of crowded shoots. Thereafter, reduce main stems by one third, sideshoots to 2–3 buds and remove unproductive shoots.
	Mid-autumn	Cut back tall stems, if needed, to keep the shrub tidy.
Leptospermum (tea tree) ES	Mid-spring	A light trim for shape is all a specimen shrub needs. If wall-trained, remove misplaced shoots and cut back long stems to within bounds.
Leycesteria formosa (Himalayan honeysuckle) DS	Late winter–early spring	Cut out the flowered shoots to the base every year. If the shrub gets too scruffy, coppice it by chopping all the canes to 5–8cm (2–3in) above soil level; a fresh batch will spring up in no time.
Ligustrum (privet) ES	Late winter–early spring	Prune shrubs to remove crossing or crowded shoots or cut back hard to renovate gappy or old plants.
	Late spring–early autumn	Shear hedges and topiary every 6 weeks in the growing season.
Liquidambar styraciflua (sweet gum) DT	Late winter–early spring	Cut out crossing or misplaced branches. No other pruning is required on this elegant tree.
Liriodendron tulipifera (tulip tree) DT	Late winter–early spring	No regular pruning is necessary.
Lomatia ET	Midsummer–late summer, after flowering	Prune simply to maintain an open canopy, taking out crossing or badly placed branches. Wall-trained plants, with 3–5 main stems from a 30cm (12in) base, need little pruning, but shorten over-long stems.
Lonicera (honeysuckle) *L. henryi, L. japonica, L. periclymenum* ECL	Late winter–spring, after risk of frost is past	Prune long stems to keep them within bounds. If you have ended up with a large tangle of stems, take drastic action: hack it off with a hedge trimmer to leave just 60–90cm (2–3ft) at the base.
L. nitida ES	Late spring–early autumn	This lax shrub needs a lot of pruning, otherwise it can develop a 'drunken' habit. To maintain a formal hedge or topiary, remove half of the new growth every 6 weeks during the growing season.
L. fragrantissima, L. maackii, L. × purpusii DS	Late spring, after flowering	Cut back weak and old shoots to the base. Prune one third of stems to an upright shoot, without spoiling the overall shape.
Magnolia Deciduous types	Late summer (to avoid bleeding)	Regular pruning is unnecessary, but dead-head and trim frost-damaged tips. Most deciduous magnolias don't like being pruned, but their brittle stems sometimes suffer damage – phase renovation of unbalanced plants over 2–3 years.
M. grandiflora ES	Late summer–early winter	After planting, remove tips of competing leaders, and in early years trim sideshoots for bushy growth.
	Spring	Trim off frost damage on established shrubs.
Mahonia ES	Mid-spring, after flowering or – to keep berries – in the following year, before new stems flower	Needs little or no pruning, apart from taking out any unhealthy or spindly growth. If the 'leg' looks sparse, cut a few old stems out at the base to prompt new growth. Prune a straggly specimen hard to renovate.

Plant name	When to prune	How to prune
Malus (crab apple) DT	Late winter–early spring, after flowering	Prune young trees to achieve an open, balanced canopy. Little pruning is needed otherwise, but remove suckers.
Michelia ET	Spring, as growth begins	These frost-tender trees don't react well to hard pruning; lightly shape them or cut back over-long shoots to within the body of the plant.
Morus (mulberry) DT	Late autumn–early winter (to avoid bleeding)	Limit pruning to essential maintenance, such as cutting out crossing or dead stems and clearing water shoots.
Myrica M. californica (California wax myrtle) ES	Spring	Minimal pruning: cut out any crossing or wayward stems and any frost-damaged growth to live wood.
M. gale (bog myrtle, sweet gale) DS	Spring	The only pruning needed is a light trim; if any stems become leggy, cut them down to ground level.
Myrtus communis (myrtle) ES	Late winter–early spring	On wall-trained shrubs, reduce all flowered shoots to 2–4 buds from the main stems.
	Mid-spring–late spring	Lightly trim hedges and cut back any wayward shoots.
Nandina domestica (heavenly bamboo) ES	Mid-spring	Little pruning is necessary. Remove dead or weak shoots. Renovate by cutting out old stems to the base over several years.
Nerium oleander (oleander) ES	Late summer–autumn	Cut back flowered shoots by half and sideshoots to 10cm (4in). Trim wayward or unhealthy shoots on standards to create a balanced head. Beware of the toxic sap – wear gloves.
Nothofagus ET/DT	Late winter–early spring	Remove wayward or crossing stems. Some species may develop heavy 'skirts' of lower branches, which throw out long sub-laterals or begin curving upwards at the perimeter.
Nyssa (tupelo) DT	Autumn–early spring	These are often grown as multi-stemmed trees to display the richly hued leaves. Lightly prune to maintain the overall shape by cutting out misplaced or crossing branches.
Olearia (daisy bush) ES	Early spring, once new growth begins, or late summer, after flowering	Cut back frost-damaged shoots to healthy buds and cut out spent flowering stems. Trim hedges and topiary after flowering. This bush responds well to hard pruning; to restrict the spread, cut back last year's shoots by a half to one third.
Osmanthus ES	Late spring–early summer, after flowering	These look best if left to grow naturally, even if wall-trained. Cut the longest stems to within the body of the hedge to hide the truncated shoots and cut out spent flowering stems. Clip hedges and topiary once or twice before midsummer. Hard prune neglected shrubs.
Paeonia (tree peony) DS	Summer, after flowering, or in autumn, after leaf fall	Cut spent flowering shoots back to new sideshoots. Avoid drastic pruning, but take out a few old, leggy stems at the base occasionally.
Parrotia (Persian ironwood) DT	Autumn–early spring	These may adopt a tree-like or shrubby habit: in either case, it is generally best to leave them alone. Thin out crowded branches in young trees to create an open canopy. Take out any suckers.
Parthenocissus (Virginia creeper, Boston ivy) DCL	Autumn–early winter	Train young plants onto a sturdy support. Once they have clung on, trim lightly with shears and keep them clear of gutters and roofs. Chop right back to within 1m (40in) to renovate.
Passiflora ECL	Spring	Remove weak and crowded shoots and cut back long shoots to the allotted space. Don't prune too hard, to maintain flowering.
	After flowering	Reduce flowered shoots to 2–3 buds of the framework to create spurs.
Paulownia tomentosa (foxglove tree) DT	Early–mid-spring	This quickly forms an open tree with large flower spikes before the leaves. It needs little pruning, but coppicing each year will produce an umbrella of huge, velvety leaves. Chop stems to 15cm (6in) each year.
Perovskia atriplicifolia (Russian sage) DS	Spring, just after the buds burst	The stems die back each winter but you can build up a sturdy, woody framework of stems by pruning the woody base each year. Cut all the stems hard back to 15–30cm (6–12in) and 1–2 buds.

Plant name	When to prune	How to prune
Philadelphus (mock orange) DS	Midsummer, after flowering	Cut no more than one fifth of the oldest stems to 5–8cm (2–3in) above soil level each year to refresh the growth and keep tidy. Choose a cultivar of the right size for the space; it won't like severe pruning.
Phillyrea latifolia ES	Mid-spring	Lightly shape by cutting back wayward or crowded shoots.
	Midsummer	If growing this as topiary, lightly trim after flowering.
Phlomis ES	Mid-spring, after growth begins	Regular pruning is not needed, but cut back to healthy buds to reshape and refresh older, untidy shrubs. Take out old and weak shoots entirely, and shorten leggy stems to within the body of the bush.
Phoenix canariensis (Canary date palm) ES	When necessary	No regular pruning is needed, but cut off dead or damaged leaves towards the base. Don't cut into the trunk; leave a neat stub.
Photinia ES	Spring, after flowering	Remove thin shoots, cut back by one third any over-long stems, and shorten the remaining stems by up to 15cm (6in) to get a handsome flush of young, scarlet foliage in the following year.
	Summer	Trim hedges again when the young foliage has faded.
Phygelius ES	Spring, after buds burst and risk of frost is past	These are often cut back naturally by frost. Prune the woody base to 15–30cm (6–12in) and 1–2 buds on each stem, or below frost-damaged growth, to encourage the green shoots of recovery.
Picea (spruce) ET/ES	Late spring–midsummer	Check young plants and cut out any competing leaders. Pruning is not usually required on mature conifers, but shoots, or 'candles', can be cut down by half while still soft to keep the plant bushy. As with most conifers, don't cut into old wood.
Pieris ES	Spring, after flowering	In the first 3 years, remove weak and crossing branches to create an open framework. Thereafter, remove thin shoots, cut back by one third or to an upright shoot, dead-head, and shorten stems by up to 15cm (6in) for a good crop of scarlet foliage next year.
Pinus ET	Late spring–midsummer	Prune as for *Picea*. If the leading shoot is damaged, remove all but the strongest of the vertical shoots below, to coax along its replacement.
Pittosporum ES	Mid-spring, after growth begins, and midsummer	Trim wayward shoots or crossing stems. Most naturally grow with a single stem: cut back all the lowest sideshoots to create a standard. Trim hedges again in midsummer.
Populus (aspen, poplar) DT	Summer	Avoid pruning – some poplars bleed badly and others are vulnerable to canker. However, remove any water shoots or suckers.
Potentilla fruticosa (cinquefoil) DS	Mid-spring	Clear out twiggy, old growth, cutting it back to the base and shorten strong new shoots by up to a half, to keep the plant compact.
	Autumn	Shear off spent flowering stems to within 2.5cm (1in) of the old wood.
Prunus (most ornamental cherries) DT	Midsummer, after flowering	Don't risk pruning except when the sap is flowing freely: the bleeding sap stops silver leaf disease entering the wounds. Keep cuts to a minimum, removing badly placed or crossing branches, and suckers.
P. × cistena, P. incisa, P. tenella DS	Late spring, after flowering	Regular pruning is unnecessary, unless these are grown as dense hedges. Then, use secateurs to shape after the flowers fade.
P. glandulosa, P. triloba DS	Late spring, after flowering	These may be grown in the border or against a wall. Prune harder than most ornamental cherries: cut all stems to 2–3 buds within the main framework.
P. laurocerasus (cherry laurel), *P. lusitanica* (Portugal laurel) ES	Mid-spring	Remove any thin shoots and cut back by one third any over-long stems. Dead-head after flowering. Cut formal hedges hard back with secateurs; if needed, renovate them by cutting down to the base.
	Late summer	Trim long shoots by one third.
Ptelea trifoliata (hop tree, water ash) DS	Early–mid-spring	Regular pruning is not necessary, but cut hard back to curtail its spreading habit. You can also train this shrub as a standard.

Plant name	When to prune	How to prune
Pterocarya (wing nut) DT	Late winter (never in autumn)	Pendulous lower branches may root and branch into a tangle; remove them completely, if necessary.
	Winter–late summer	Remove suckers as and when you spot them – removing them all once a year will encourage an even bigger crop.
Pyracantha (firethorn) ES	Spring	Prune wall-trained shrubs by cutting out unproductive stems and pruning to shape. Rejuvenate by hard renewal pruning.
	Midsummer	Trim hedges.
	Late summer	Shorten all new sideshoots on shrubs to 2–3 leaves to get a better crop of flower buds the following year, and to expose this year's berries. Take care not to remove stems with developing buds.
Pyrus (ornamental pear) DT	Autumn–early spring	These trees resent hard pruning; restrict to light trimming or thinning.
Quercus (oak) ET/ DT	Winter	Even the smaller garden oaks need little pruning, except to remove dead wood.
Rhododendron Deciduous types (azaleas)	Late winter–early spring	Keep tall azaleas in check with occasional pruning; cut out misplaced or crossing shoots to keep a balanced shape.
Evergreen types	Mid-spring	Remove thin shoots and cut back over-long stems by one third. Hard prune into old wood to renovate sprawling or aged shrubs, but not grafted shrubs or those with peeling bark. Remove suckers.
	Early summer, after flowering	Dead-head by snapping the flowerheads at the base, taking care not to damage the new buds just below.
Rhus typhina (sumach) DS	Late winter–early spring	Regular pruning is unnecessary and might encourage suckering; cut or mow off any suckers as soon as they pop up.
Ribes sanguineum (flowering currant) DS	Mid–late spring, after flowering	Cut one fifth of oldest stems to 5–8cm (2–3in) above soil level to keep established shrubs and hedges looking jaunty, and cut down each flowered shoot to a young sideshoot that hasn't flowered. If the plant gets too big, you can clip it quite heavily to keep it smaller.
Robinia pseudoacacia (false acacia, locust) DT	Midsummer–late summer	Prune as little as possible: wounds don't heal well and the tree may react by sending out lots of vertical stems. Remove suckers promptly.
Rosa (rose) *R. sericea* f. *pteracantha* DS	Late winter–early spring	In the second year, coppice to make the most of its colourful stems and thorns by cutting all stems to 5–8cm (2–3in) above soil level. Repeat every other year.
Cluster-flowered bush rose (floribunda) DS	Late winter–early spring	Remove unhealthy growth and any crossing shoots to leave an open centre. Cut the main stems down to 25–30cm (10–12in) and the remaining sideshoots by about half of their length.
	Throughout growing season	Dead-head to prolong flowering. Remove suckers as soon as seen.
Large-flowered bush rose (hybrid tea) DS	Late winter–early spring	Remove unhealthy growth and any crossing shoots to leave an open centre. Cut the main stems down to 15–20cm (6–8in).
	Throughout growing season	Dead-head to prolong flowering. Remove suckers as soon as seen.
Modern shrub and species rose DS	Late winter–early spring	Lightly prune, taking out 2–3 old stems at the base and remaining stem tips to encourage flowering. *R. rugosa* may be grown as an informal hedge.
	Throughout growing season	Dead-head to prolong flowering, unless you want to enjoy a display of rosehips. Remove suckers as soon as seen.
Miniature and patio rose DS	Late winter–early spring	Thin out crowded stems and trim remaining shoots by up to one third. Reduce over-long shoots as necessary.
	Throughout growing season	Dead-head by shearing after each flush. Remove suckers when seen.

Plant name	When to prune	How to prune
Climbing rose DCL	Late winter–early spring	Cut out unhealthy and crowded growth at the base; reduce sideshoots by two thirds; tie in most of the stems horizontally, to prompt more flower buds to break, and allow the central ones to continue upwards. Remove any unruly shoots.
	Throughout growing season	Dead-head to prolong flowering. Remove suckers as soon as seen.
Rambling rose DCL	Late summer, after flowering	Cut out a quarter of the stems, targeting old, tired shoots, to encourage vigorous, new stems to grow up. After tying in remaining young shoots, cut their sideshoots back to 2–3 buds to form flowering spurs.
	Throughout growing season	Remove suckers as soon as seen.
Alba, damask, gallica, moss roses DS	Summer, after flowering	Cut 2–3 old stems to the base and lightly prune the other stems by at least a quarter. Reduce sideshoots by up to a half or to the main stem on gallica roses.
Rosmarinus officinalis (rosemary) ES	Late summer	Clip over topiary or dwarf hedges.
Rubus biflorus, R. cockburnianus, R. thibetanus (ornamental bramble) DS	Late winter–early spring	To show off the spectacular colour of the young stems, coppice each year by cutting all stems to 5–8cm (2–3in) above soil level. This also curtails the rampant, spreading habit of the plants.
Ruscus aculeatus (butcher's broom) ES	Mid-spring	This needs little or no pruning, apart from taking out any unhealthy or spindly growth.
Ruta (rue) ES	Early spring	The blue-grey leaves are the best feature of these sub-shrubs, so don't bother with the flowers. Cut back the entire plant by half (into the old wood) for lush foliage and a compact shape. Even harder pruning, to 15cm (6in), will rejuvenate neglected plants.
Salix S. alba, S. daphnoides, S. hookeriana (willow) DT/DS	Early–mid-spring	This group of willows are often coppiced, to show off their colourful stems, or keep them as shrubs instead of trees. Cut all stems to 5–8cm (2–3in) above soil level. Pollard them by reducing stems in the same way, but to a central stem of 60–150cm (2–5ft). The prunings make useful willow wands for weaving.
S. caprea 'Kilmarnock' (Kilmarnock willow) DT	Autumn–winter	Cut out completely all dead stems from beneath the crown, to open up the weeping canopy and keep it free of disease.
Salvia officinalis (sage) ES	Spring, as growth begins	Prune out weak shoots at the base to encourage new growth.
Sambucus (elder) DS	Early summer	After flowering, shear off spent shoots.
	Winter, while dormant	Cut down to get a good crop of coloured foliage. Cut last year's stems to within 15cm (6in) of the main branches, so the plant is only waist-high, or coppice by cutting all stems to 5–8cm (2–3in) above soil level. With cultivars grown for flowers, prune more lightly to shape.
Santolina chamaecyparissus (cotton lavender) ES	Mid- or late spring–early summer	As growth begins, prune out weak shoots at the base to encourage new growth – don't hard prune into old wood. Clip dwarf hedges.
	Late summer, after flowering	Shear off spent shoots.
Sarcococca (Christmas box, sweet box) ES	Spring	Pruning is minimal: reshape by cutting back any wayward stems, but don't prune too heavily – otherwise, next year's flowering will suffer.
Schefflera ES	Late winter–early spring	Regular pruning is not required – maintain a balanced shape by cutting out crossing or awkwardly placed stems.
Schizophragma DCL	Spring	Plants scrambling through trees or over large walls need little pruning. Wall-trained plants sometimes throw out long, soft shoots without flower buds; cut these out completely. Prune to keep within bounds.
Skimmia ES	Spring, after flowering	These are naturally compact so don't need regular pruning. If needed, cut unbalanced, long stems back to within the shrub.

Plant name	When to prune	How to prune
Solanum crispum (Chilean potato tree) ECL	Early spring	Remove unwanted growth each year and reduce sideshoots to within 2–3 buds of the main stems. Renovation should be phased if it is to work: take out one stem at the base each year to renew the plant.
Sophora (kowhai) ET/DT/ES/DS	Midsummer (to avoid bleeding)	Avoid pruning if possible. In cold areas, the plant may need the protection of training against a wall.
Sorbus (mountain ash, rowan, whitebeam) DT/DS	Autumn–early spring	Remove misplaced or crossing shoots and suckers that appear on trunks of grafted forms.
Sparrmannia africana (African hemp) ET/ES	Winter	Cut back hard – annually or every other year – to a low framework or even larger leaves and flowers, or to ground level to renovate.
	Summer	Alternatively, lightly prune any shoots that mar the natural shape.
Spartium junceum (Spanish broom) DS	Early spring, when growth begins	In the second spring, reduce the new growth by half, cut out all weak stems and one-third of crowded shoots. Thereafter, reduce main stems by one third, sideshoots to 2–3 buds and completely remove old, unproductive shoots. This should encourage flowering.
Spiraea S. 'Arguta' DS	Early summer, after flowering	Like many spiraeas that flower on old wood, this needs regular pruning to keep it flowering at its best. Shorten flowered shoots back to strong buds and remove up to one quarter of the stems at the base.
S. *japonica* DS	Early spring	This flowers on new wood – build a low framework of 15cm (6in) stems on young plants, then cut back all stems to within 1–2 buds of it every year.
Stachyurus praecox DT/DS	Spring, after flowering	Regular pruning is unnecessary, apart from occasionally shortening long shoots to keep the shape.
Stephanandra DS	Summer, after flowering	Renew the suckering clump by removing up to one quarter of the stems at the base and shortening flowered shoots to good sideshoots, without impairing the arching habit.
Stephanotis ECL	Late winter–early spring	Keep the bushy habit by cutting back weak and crowded shoots, as well as shortening long, stray stems. Tie in new stems to the support.
Styrax (snowbell) DS	Late winter–early spring	Regular pruning is unnecessary.
Symphoricarpos (snowberry) DS	Late winter–early spring	Thin old, twiggy growth and, if you need it to be a more manageable size, cut down the flowered stems to strong, new shoots on the plant.
Syringa vulgaris (lilac) DS	Midsummer, after flowering	Regular pruning is unnecessary; dead-head, taking care not to damage new shoots below the flowers, and remove suckers promptly.
	Winter	Rejuvenate older shrubs by hard pruning one third of the stems to 30–60cm (12–24in) each year over three years.
S. *meyeri*, S. *microphylla*	Midsummer, after flowering	Naturally twiggy plants don't need much pruning.
Tamarix (tamarisk) T. *ramosissima* DS	Late winter–early spring	In the second spring, reduce the new growth by half and cut out one third of crowded shoots. Thereafter, reduce main stems by one third and sideshoots to 2–3 buds; remove old, unproductive shoots.
T. *tetrandra* DS	Spring, after flowering	Cut back stems to strong buds or sideshoot by a half to two thirds.
Taxus baccata (yew) ET/ES	Late spring–early summer	This classic hedging loves hard pruning. For a really crisp outline, trim it first at the beginning of the season.
	Late summer–early autumn	Clip formal hedges and topiary again to maintain a clear shape.
	Autumn–early winter	Renovate neglected or over-sized hedges by cutting back hard on one side, then do the same to the other side in the following year.
Thuja plicata (Western red cedar) ET	Late spring and late summer–early autumn	Trim twice, without cutting into old wood. Single trees need no pruning, except to remove competing leaders.

Plant name	When to prune	How to prune
Thymus ES	Late summer	Harvest sprigs constantly by pinch pruning to keep the foliage fresh, but shearing over the spent flowered stems also does the trick. Cut out reverted green shoots on variegated forms before they take over.
Tibouchina ES	Spring	Tip-prune young shoots to make them bush out. Cut back flowered stems to 2 pairs of buds to encourage new growth.
Tilia (lime, linden) DT	Midsummer–midwinter (to avoid bleeding)	These trees react well to heavy pruning, so are often pollarded or even pleached. Remove suckers as they appear. Mature, untrained trees are prone to problems such as dieback, unbalanced crowns and heavy limbs that distort the canopy.
Trachelospermum jasminoides (star jasmine) ECL	Late winter–spring, when risk of frost is past	Train this tender climber over a sheltered pergola or up a wall. Prune lightly, cutting weak shoots to strong buds and old stems to the base. Lop off two thirds of the plant to renovate.
Trachycarpus fortunei (Chusan palm) ET	When necessary	No regular pruning needed, but cut off dead or damaged leaves towards the base.
Ulex (gorse) ES	Mid-spring or after flowering	Clip over lightly after flowering. If necessary, cut all the stems back hard to within 15cm (6in) of the ground in spring.
Ulmus (elm) DT	Autumn–early spring	Regular pruning is not necessary, although some species tend to drop dead branches suddenly, so keep an eye out for dying stems and get a professional to remove them. Some elms also throw out water shoots or suckers, which need removing promptly.
Vestia foetida ES	Midsummer, after flowering	Dead-head and trim lightly, cutting out over-long or crossing shoots.
Viburnum ES/DS		Regular pruning is not needed, but cut out crowded, over-long or crossing stems from time to time. Some evergreens respond well to training as standards or hedges.
	Spring	Prune winter-flowering deciduous species, if needed. Thin evergreens.
	Midsummer	Prune summer-flowering deciduous species, if needed.
Vinca (periwinkle) ES	Early–mid-spring	Periwinkle naturally sprawl and scramble, but pruning prevents them from looking less messy. Cut back excessively long stems or, if the plant is very tangled, shear the entire surface of the plant.
Vitex DT/DS	Spring	Cut flowered stems hard back to healthy lower shoots; to create spurs, remove a stem or two at the base. On a wall-trained shrub, shorten all last year's shoots to 2–4 buds. Tie in a new shoot to fill the frame.
Vitis coignetiae (ornamental vine) DCL	Winter and summer	Thin out unwanted stems and shorten long leaders. On formally trained vines, reduce each flowered shoot 2–3 buds from the main stems.
Weigela DS	Midsummer, after flowering	Shorten flowered shoots to healthy buds or sideshoots. Cut a quarter of oldest stems to 5–8cm (2–3in) above soil level to stimulate foliage growth. For flowers, take out 1–2 old stems each year.
Wisteria	Late summer	For formative pruning, *see* page 75. After flowering, cut back sideshoots to 15–20cm (6–8in) or 5–7 leaves from the main stem.
	Late winter	Shorten the sideshoots pruned in summer back to 2–3 strong buds to form flowering spurs. Shorten secondary shoots to 15–20cm (6–8in).
Yucca filamentosa ES	Spring, when risk of frost is past	Cut damaged branches back to just above new shoots. To stimulate new growth, cut hard back to low sideshoots or basal shoots. Cut out spent flower spikes by cutting close to the centre of the rosette.
Zelkova abelicea DT	Late winter	Prune only to remove badly placed branches.

Index

Acknowledgements

BBC and Outhouse would like to thank the following for their assistance in preparing this book: Candida Frith-Macdonald and Andrew McIndoe for their advice and guidance; Annelise Evans for research; Louise Turpin for design assistance; Joanne Forrest Smith for picture research; Helena Caldon for proofreading; June Wilkins for the index.

Picture credits

Key t = top; b = bottom; l = left; r = right; c = centre

All photographs by Jonathan Buckley except the following:
Alamy/Lifestyle David J Green 25. **DK Images** 114. **GAP Photos** Elke Borkowski 106. Geoff du Feu 117. FhF Greenmedia 27, 49. Jerry Harpur 90. Dianna Jazwinski 97. S&O Matthews 16. Howard Rice 24bl, 42r. JS Sira 121. Maddie Thornhill 22t. Vision 39b. Jo Whitworth 123. Rob Whitworth 120. **Marianne Majerus** 24t. **Harpur Garden Library** 22bl. **Clive Nichols** 37t. **Science Photo Library** Malcolm Thomas 20.

Thanks are also due to the following designers and owners whose gardens appear in the book:

Rosemary Alexander, Stoneacre, Kent 67t. Maureen Allen, St John's Road, Walsall 50. Beth Chatto, Beth Chatto Gardens, Essex 11t. Coughton Court, Warwickshire 84t. Judith Glover, RHS Chelsea Flower Show 2003 69b. Anthony Goff 2–3. Graham Gough, Marchants Hardy Plants, East Sussex 61. Bunny Guinness 104b. Anthea Guthrie 121. Simon Hopkinson 89b, 91. Roy and Barbara Joseph, The Dingle, Powys 44b, 47. Rani Lall 8, 65, 69t, 87. Christopher Lloyd, Great Dixter, East Sussex 11b, 12t, 17, 34, 43l, 80. John Massey, Ashwood Nurseries, Staffordshire 29, 32, 34, 35t, 45, 62. Mr and Mrs Mogford 21b, 42r. Anthony Noel 71. Dan Pearson 37b. Faith Raven, Docwras Manor, Hertfordshire 70. Sarah Raven, Perch Hill, East Sussex 26, 42l. Elaine Rolfe, Ochran Mill, Gwent 90. Diana Ross 79r. David and Mavis Seeney 78. Carol and Malcolm Skinner, Eastgrove Cottage Garden Nursery, Worcestershire 65b. Sue and Wol Staines, Glen Chantry, Essex 21t. Joe Swift and Sam Joyce for The Plant Room 43r. Raymond Treasure and Gordon Fenn, Stockton Bury, Herefordshire 33. West Dean Gardens, West Sussex 95, 108b. Helen Yemm, Ketley's, East Sussex 48.